HD58.6 .H37 2000

Harvard business r
on negotiation an
c2000.

D0055920

2001 11 12

0 1341 0425363 5

Harvard Business Review

ON
NEGOTIATION AND
CONFLICT RESOLUTION

THE HARVARD BUSINESS REVIEW PAPERBACK SERIES

The series is designed to bring today's managers and professionals the fundamental information they need to stay competitive in a fast-moving world. From the preeminent thinkers whose work has defined an entire field to the rising stars who will redefine the way we think about business, here are the leading minds and landmark ideas that have established the *Harvard Business Review* as required reading for ambitious businesspeople in organizations around the globe.

Other books in the series:

Harvard Business Review on Brand Management

Harvard Business Review on Breakthrough Thinking

Harvard Business Review on Business and the Environment

Harvard Business Review on the Business Value of IT

Harvard Business Review on Change

Harvard Business Review on Corporate Governance

Harvard Business Review on Corporate Strategy

Harvard Business Review on Crisis Management

Harvard Business Review on Effective Communication

Harvard Business Review on Entrepreneurship

Harvard Business Review on Knowledge Management

Harvard Business Review on Leadership

Harvard Business Review on Managing High-Tech Industries

Harvard Business Review on Managing People

Harvard Business Review on Managing Uncertainty

Harvard Business Review on Managing the Value Chain

Harvard Business Review on Measuring Corporate Performance

Harvard Business Review on Nonprofits

Harvard Business Review on Strategies for Growth

Harvard
Business
Review

ON

NEGOTIATION AND
CONFLICT RESOLUTION

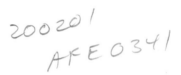

A HARVARD BUSINESS REVIEW PAPERBACK

NIAGARA COLLEGE LRC

Copyright 1960, 1984, 1988, 1990, 1994, 1997, 1999, 2000
President and Fellows of Harvard College
All rights reserved
Printed in the United States of America
04 03 02 01 00   5 4 3 2 1

All rights reserved. No part of this book may be reproduced, stored in a
retrieval system, or transmitted, in any form or by any means, electronic, mechanical, photocopying, recording, or otherwise without the
prior written permission of the copyright holder.

The *Harvard Business Review* articles in this collection are available as
individual reprints. Discounts apply to quantity purchases. For information and ordering, please contact Customer Service, Harvard Business
School Publishing, Boston, MA 02163. Telephone: (617) 783-7500 or
(800) 988-0886, 8 A.M. to 6 P.M. Eastern Time, Monday through Friday.
Fax: (617) 783-7555, 24 hours a day. E-mail: custserv@hbsp.harvard.edu.

Library of Congress Cataloging-in-Publication Data
Harvard business review on negotiation and conflict resolution.
      p.   cm. — (Harvard business review paperback series)
    Includes index.
    ISBN 1-57851-236-0 (alk. paper)
    1. Negotiation in business.   2. Conflict management.   I. Harvard
business review.   II. Title: Negotiation and conflict resolution.
III. Series.
HD58.6.H383 2000
658.4′05—dc21   99-28453
                                       CIP

*The paper used in this publication meets the requirements of the Ameri-
can National Standard for Permanence of Paper for Publications and
Documents in Libraries and Archives Z39.48-1992.*

Contents

Harvard
Business
Review

ON

NEGOTIATION AND
CONFLICT RESOLUTION

Management of Differences

WARREN H. SCHMIDT AND
ROBERT TANNENBAUM

Executive Summary

WHEN DIFFERENCES AMONG PEOPLE cause feelings to run high, managers need to understand the nature of these differences in order to deal with them systematically and in such a way that both corporate harmony and individual initiative are preserved.

THE MANAGER OFTEN experiences his most uncomfortable moments when he has to deal with differences among people. Because of these differences, he must often face disagreements, arguments, and even open conflict. To add to his discomfort, he frequently finds himself torn by two opposing desires. On the one hand, he wants to unleash the individuality of his subordinates in order to tap their full potential and to achieve novel and creative approaches to problems. On the other hand, he is eager to develop a harmonious, smooth-working team to carry out his organization's objectives. The manager's lot is further troubled by the fact that when differences do occur, strong feelings are frequently aroused, objectivity flies out the window, egos are threatened, and personal relationships are placed in jeopardy.

Toward Effective Management

Because the presence of differences can complicate the manager's job in so many ways, it is of utmost importance that he understand them fully and that he learn to handle them effectively. It is the purpose of this article to assist the manager to manage more effectively by increasing his understanding of differences among the people he works with, and by improving his ability to deal with others.

A large part of what follows will focus, for simplicity of exposition, on the differences which occur among a manager's individual subordinates. However, we would like to suggest that the principles, concepts, methods, and dynamics which we discuss throughout much of the article apply to intergroup, to interorganizational, and to international differences as well.

Our basic thesis is that a manager's ability to deal effectively with differences depends on:

- His ability to diagnose and to understand differences.

- His awareness of, and ability to select appropriately from, a variety of behaviors.[1]

- His awareness of, and ability to deal with, his own

feelings—particularly those which might reduce his social sensitivity (diagnostic insight) and his action flexibility (ability to act appropriately).[2]

There are two basic assumptions underlying our approach to this problem. Let us examine them before going any further:

1. **Differences among people should not be regarded as inherently "good" or "bad."** Sometimes differences result in important benefits to the organization; and sometimes they are disruptive, reducing the overall effectiveness of individuals and organizations.

2. **There is no one "right" way to deal with differences.** Under varying circumstances, it may be most beneficial to avoid differences, to repress them, to sharpen them into clearly defined conflict, or to utilize them for enriched problem solving. The manager who consistently "pours oil on troubled waters" may not be the most effective manager. Nor is the manager necessarily successful who emphasizes individuality and differences so strongly that cooperation and teamwork are simply afterthoughts. We feel, rather, that the effective manager is one who is able to use a *variety* of approaches to differences and who chooses any specific approach on the basis of an insightful diagnosis and understanding of the factors with which he is faced at that time.

Diagnosing Disagreements

When a manager's subordinates become involved in a heated disagreement, they do not tend to proceed in a systematic manner to resolve their difference. The issues often remain unclear to them, and they may talk *at* rather than *to* one another. If a manager is to be helpful in such a situation, he should ask three important diagnostic questions:

1. What is the nature of the difference among the persons?

2. What factors may underlie this difference?

3. To what stage has the interpersonal difference evolved?

NATURE OF THE DIFFERENCE

Now, looking at the first of these three important questions, the nature of the difference will vary depending on the kind of issue on which people disagree. And there are four basic kinds of issues to look for:

• **Facts.** Sometimes the disagreement occurs because individuals have different definitions of a problem, are aware of different pieces of relevant information, accept or reject different information as factual, or have differing impressions of their respective power and authority.

• **Goals.** Sometimes the disagreement is about what should be accomplished—the desirable objectives of a department, division, section, or of a specific position within the organization.

• **Methods.** Sometimes individuals differ about the procedures, strategies, or tactics which would most likely achieve a mutually desired goal.

• **Values.** Sometimes the disagreement is over ethics—the way power should be exercised, or moral considerations, or assumptions about justice, fairness, and so on. Such differences may affect the choice of either goals or methods.

Arguments are prolonged and confusion is increased when the contending parties are not sure of the nature of the issue over which they disagree. By discovering the source of the disagreement, the manager will be in a better position to determine how he can utilize and direct the dispute for both the short- and long-range good of the organization. As we will indicate later, there are certain steps which are appropriate when the differences are about facts, other steps which are appropriate when the differences are over goals, and still other steps which are applicable when differences are over methods or values.

UNDERLYING FACTORS

When people are faced with a difference, it is not enough that their manager be concerned with what the difference is about. The second major diagnostic question he should ask is *why* the difference exists. As we try to discover useful answers to this, it is helpful to think in terms of:

- Whether the disputants had access to the same information.

- Whether the disputants perceive the common information differently.

- Whether each disputant is significantly influenced by his role in the organization.

These questions involve informational, perceptual, and role factors. Thus:

Informational factors exert their influence when the various points of view have developed on the basis of different sets of facts. The ancient legend of the blind men and the elephant dramatizes this point as vividly as any modern illustration. Because each of the men had contact with a different part of the elephant, each disagreed violently about the nature of the animal. In the same way, when two persons receive limited information about a complex problem, they may well disagree as to the nature of that problem when they come together to solve it.

Perceptual factors exert their influence when the persons have different images of the same stimulus. Each will attend to, and select from the information available, those items which he deems important. Each will interpret the information in a somewhat different manner. Each brings to the data a different set of life experiences which cause him to view the information through a highly personal kind of filter. The picture which he gets, therefore, is unique to him. Thus it is not surprising that the same basic "facts" may produce distinctive perceptual pictures in the minds of different individuals.

Role factors exert their influence because each of the individuals occupies a certain position and status in society or in the organization. The fact that he occupies such a position or status may put certain constraints on him if the discussion is related to his role.

The concepts we have been discussing can be best illustrated by a concrete case. Such a case is presented in detail in the exhibit "Hypothetical Situation Illustrating a Difference."

STAGE OF EVOLUTION

Important conflicts among people ordinarily do not erupt suddenly. They pass through various stages, and the way in which the energy of the disputing parties can be effectively directed by the manager depends to some extent on the stage of the dispute when he enters the picture.

One way of diagnosing a dispute—the third major question—is to identify it as being at one of these five stages in its development:

Stage #1—the phase of anticipation. A manager learns that his company is about to install new, automated equipment which will reduce the number and change the nature of jobs in a given department. He can anticipate that when this information is released, there will be differences of opinion as to the desirability of this change, the way in which it should be introduced, and the way in which the consequences of its introduction should be handled.

Stage #2—the phase of conscious, but unexpressed, difference. Word leaks out about the proposed new equipment. Small clusters of people who trust one another begin discussing it. They have no definite basis for the information, but tensions begin to build up within the organization. There is a feeling of impending dispute and trouble.

Stage #3—the phase of discussion. Information is presented about the plans to install new equipment. Questions are asked to secure more information, to inquire about the intentions of management, to test the firmness of the decision that has been made. During the discussion, the differing opinions of individuals begin to emerge openly. They are implied by the questions which are asked, and by the language which is used.

Stage #4—the phase of open dispute. The union steward meets with the foreman to present arguments for a

Hypothetical Situation Illustrating a Difference

THE FACTS

There is a disagreement over whether a company should introduce automated record keeping to replace its present manual system. The company's expert on office methods favors immediate introduction of such a system. The head of accounting is opposed to it. Some of the bases of disagreement and possible reasons for the disagreement are represented below.

NATURE OF THE DIFFERENCE

	Over facts	Over methods	Over goals	Over values
Expert on office methods	"Automation will save the company money."	"The new system should be installed fully and at once."	"We want a system that gives us accurate data rapidly—whenever we want it."	"We must be modern and efficient."
Head of accounting department	"The new system will be more expensive to install and operate."	"Let us move slower—one step at a time."	"We need most a flexible accounting system to meet our changing needs—managed by accountants who can solve unexpected and complex problems."	"We must consider the welfare of workers who have served the company so loyally for many years."

REASONS FOR THE DIFFERENCE

	Explanation of position of methods expert	Explanation of position of head accountant
Informational (exposure to different information)	He has studied articles about seemingly comparable companies describing the savings brought about by automation. Representatives of machine companies have presented him with estimates of savings over a 10-year period.	He has heard about the "hidden costs" in automation. He has priced the kind of equipment he believes will be necessary and has estimated depreciation. This estimated cost is much higher than the salaries of possible replaced workers.
Perceptual (different interpretation of the same data because of differing backgrounds, experience, and so forth)	He regards the representatives of the machine company as being alert, businesslike, and knowledgeable about the best accounting procedures. He feels that their analysis of the company's needs is dependable and to be trusted	He sees the representatives of the machine company as salesmen. Their goal is to sell machines, and their report and analysis must be read with great caution and suspicion.
Role (pressure to take a certain stand because of status or position)	He believes that the company looks to him as the expert responsible for keeping its systems up-to-date and maximally efficient.	He feels responsible for the morale and security of his team in the accounting office. He must defend their loyalty and efficiency if it is ever doubted.

change in plans. The foreman counters these arguments by presenting the reasons that led management to decide to install the equipment. The differences which have heretofore been expressed only indirectly and tentatively now sharpen into more clearly defined points of view.

Stage #5—the phase of open conflict. Individuals have firmly committed themselves to a particular position on the issue; the dispute has become clearly defined. The outcome can only be described in terms of win, lose, or compromise. Each disputant attempts not only to increase the effectiveness of his argument and his power in the situation, but also to undermine the influence of those who oppose him.

The power of the manager to intervene successfully will differ at each of these stages. He is likely to have the most influence if he enters the picture at stage #1; the least influence if he enters at stage #5. This range of possible behavior and action changes as the conflict passes through the various stages. For this reason, it is important for the manager not only to assess the nature of the given dispute and the forces affecting the individuals involved, but also to assess the stage to which the dispute has evolved.

Selecting an Approach

After the manager has diagnosed a given dispute (or a potential one) between subordinates, he is next confronted by the problem of taking action. And here there are two additional questions that it will be helpful to him to consider:

- What courses of action are available?

- What must be kept in mind in selecting the best one?

Assuming, first, a situation in which the manager has time to anticipate and plan for an impending dispute, we suggest that the general approaches typically available to him are (a) avoidance, (b) repression, (c) sharpening into conflict, and (d) transformation into problem solving. In deciding which to use, the manager's primary concern should be to select the alternative that will yield optimum benefits to the organization.

AVOIDANCE OF DIFFERENCES

It is possible for a manager to avoid the occurrence of many differences among his subordinates. He can, for example, staff his organization with people who are in substantial agreement. Some organizations select and promote individuals whose experiences are similar, who have had similar training, and who come from a similar level of society. Because of such common backgrounds, these individuals tend to see things similarly, to have common interests and objectives, and to approach problems in much the same way. A staff thus developed tends to be a very secure one: the reactions of one's fellows are both readily predictable and congenial to one's own way of thinking and doing.

The manager may also avoid differences among his subordinates by controlling certain of their interpersonal contacts. He can, for example, assign two potentially explosive individuals to different groups or physical locations, or he can choose not to raise a particularly divisive issue because it is "too hot to handle." But let us take a closer look:

When is this alternative appropriate? Some organizations depend heavily on certain kinds of conformity and agreement among their employees in order to get the work done. Political parties and religious denominational groups are perhaps extreme examples of this. If an individual holds a different point of view on a rather fundamental issue, he may become a destructive force within the organization. This approach may be especially important if he is dealing with somewhat fragile and insecure individuals. Some persons are so threatened by conflict that their ability to function effectively suffers when they operate in a climate of differences.

What are the difficulties and dangers in this approach? The manager who uses this approach consistently runs the risk of reducing the total creativity of his staff. Someone has said, "When everyone in the room thinks the same thing, no one is thinking very much." In an atmosphere in which differences are avoided, new ideas not only appear less frequently, but old ideas also are likely to go unexamined and untested. There is genuine danger of the organization's slipping unknowingly into a rut of complacency.

REPRESSION OF DIFFERENCES

Sometimes a manager is aware that certain differences exist among members of his staff, but he feels that the open expression of these differences would create unproductive dissension and reduce the total creativity of the group. He may, therefore, decide to keep these differences under cover. He may do this by continually emphasizing loyalty, cooperation, teamwork, and other similar values within the group. In such a climate, it is unlikely that subordinates will express disagreements and risk conflict.

The manager may also try to make sure that the potentially conflicting parties come together only under circumstances which are highly controlled—circumstances in which open discussion of latent differences is clearly inappropriate. Or he may develop an atmosphere of repression by consistently rewarding agreement and cooperation and by punishing (in one way or another) those who disrupt the harmony of the organization by expressing nonconformist ideas. But once again:

When is this alternative appropriate? It is most useful when the latent differences are not relevant to the organization's task. It is to be expected that individuals will differ on many things—religion, politics, their loyalty to cities or states, baseball teams, and so forth. There may be no need to reach agreement on some of these differences in order to work together effectively on the job. It may also be appropriate to repress conflict when adequate time is not available to resolve the potential differences among the individuals involved. This might be particularly true if the manager's concern is to achieve a short-run objective and the potential disagreement is over a long-run issue. The wounds of disagreement should not be opened up if there is insufficient time to bind them.

What are the difficulties and dangers in this approach? Repression almost always costs something. If, indeed, the differences are important to the persons involved, their feelings may come to be expressed indirectly, in ways that could reduce productivity. Every manager has witnessed situations in which ideas are resisted, not on the basis of their merit, but on the basis of who advocated them. Or he has seen strong criticism arising over mistakes made by a particularly disliked individual.

Much has been said and written about "hidden agenda." People may discuss one subject, but the *way* they discuss it and the positions they take with respect to it may actually be determined by factors lying beneath the surface of the discussion. Hidden agenda are likely to abound in an atmosphere of repression.

When strong feelings are involved in unexpressed differences, the blocking of these feelings creates frustration and hostility which may be misdirected toward "safe" targets. Differences, and the feelings generated by them, do not ordinarily disappear by being ignored. They fester beneath the surface and emerge at inopportune moments to create problems for the manager and his organization.

DIFFERENCES INTO CONFLICTS

When this approach is used, the manager not only recognizes the fact that differences exist, but attempts to create an arena in which the conflicting parties can "fight it out." However, like the promoter of an athletic contest, he will want to be sure that the differing persons understand the issue over which they differ, the rules and procedures by which they can discuss their differences, and the kinds of roles and responsibilities which each is expected to bear in mind during the struggle. Again:

When is this alternative appropriate? A simple answer is: "when it is clarifying and educational." Many an individual will not pause to examine the assumptions he holds or the positions he advocates until he is called on to clarify and support them by someone who holds contrary views. In the same way, the power realities within an organization can come into sharper focus and be more commonly recognized through conflict.

For example, the manager of production and the manager of engineering may develop quite different impressions of how the board of directors feels about the relative importance of their respective units. Each is sure that the board is most impressed with the caliber of the staff, output, and operational efficiency of his department. When a dispute arises over which group is to get priority space in a new building, top management may permit both departments to exert all the influence they can on the board. During the struggle, the two managers may each gain a more realistic assessment of, and respect for, the power of the other.

Another valuable thing learned is the cost of conflict itself. Almost invariably at the end of a long dispute, there is a strong resolve that "this shall not happen again," as the individuals reflect on the financial costs, tensions, embarrassments, uneasiness, and wasted time and energy it caused.

What are the difficulties and dangers in this approach? Conflict can be very costly. It not only saps the energy of those involved, but also may irreparably destroy their future effectiveness. In the heat of conflict, words are sometimes spoken which leave lifelong scars on people or forever cloud their relationship.

Because the risks involved in conflict are so great and the potential costs so high, the manager will want to consider carefully the following questions before he uses this approach:

1. What does he hope to accomplish?

2. What are the possible outcomes of the conflict?

3. What steps should be taken to keep the conflict within organizational bounds and in perspective?

4. What can be done after the conflict to strengthen the bonds between disputants, so that the conflict will be of minimum destructiveness to them and to their ongoing relationship?

MAKING DIFFERENCES CREATIVE

"Two heads are better than one" because the two heads often represent a richer set of experiences and because they can bring to bear on the problem a greater variety of insights. If the differences are seen as enriching, rather than as in opposition to each other, the "two heads" will indeed be likely to come up with a better solution than either one alone. For example, had the six blind men who came into contact with different parts of the same elephant pooled their information, they would have arrived at a more accurate description of the animal. In the same way, many problems can be seen clearly, wholly, and in perspective only if the individuals who see different aspects can come together and pool their information. Here, too, let us take a more specific look:

When is this alternative appropriate? When it comes to choosing courses of action for a given problem, differences among the individuals in an organization can help to increase the range and variety of alternatives suggested.

The channeling of differences into a problem-solving context may also help to deal with some of the feelings which often accompany disagreement—frustration, resentment, and hostility. By providing an open and accepted approach, the manager helps to prevent undercurrents of feelings which could break out at inopportune moments. He also helps to channel the energy generated by feelings into creative, rather than into destructive, activities. Whereas conflict tends to cause individuals to seek ways of weakening and undermining those who differ with them, the problem-solving approach leads individuals to welcome differences as being potentially enriching to one's own goals, ideas, and methods.

What are the difficulties and dangers in this approach? To utilize differences requires time. Often it is easier for a single individual (rather than two or more persons) to make a decision. Also, when a rapid decision is required, it may be easier and more practical to ignore one side of an argument in order to move into action. Finally, unless a problem-solving situation is planned with some care, there is always the risk of generating conflict which will be frustrating to all parties concerned.

Enriched Problem Solving

Let us assume that the course of action decided on is the one just discussed—turning the difference into creative problem solving. Let us further assume, now, that the manager enters the picture when his subordinates are already involved in conflict. What are the things he can do if he wishes to transform this conflict into a problem-solving situation?

He can welcome the existence of differences within the organization. The manager can indicate that from the discussion of differences can come a greater variety of solutions to problems and a more adequate testing of proposed methods. By making clear his view that all parties contribute to the solution of problems by sharing their differences, he reduces the implication that there will be an ultimate "winner" and "loser."

He can listen with understanding rather than evaluation. There is abundant evidence that conflicts tend to be prolonged and to become increasingly frustrating because the conflicting parties do not really listen to one another. Each attempts to impose his own views and to "tune out" or distort what the other person has to say.

The manager may expect that when he enters the picture, the individuals will try to persuade him to take a stand on the issue involved. While each adversary is presenting his "case" to the manager, he will be watching for cues which indicate where the manager stands on the issue. It is therefore important that the manager make every effort to understand both positions as fully as possible, recognizing and supporting the seriousness of purpose of each where appropriate, and to withhold judgment until all available facts are in.

In the process of listening for understanding, the manager will also set a good example for the conflicting parties. By adopting such a listening-understanding attitude himself, and by helping the disputants to understand each other more fully, he can make a most useful contribution toward transforming potential conflict into creative problem solving.

He can clarify the nature of the conflict.   In the heat of an argument, each participant may primarily focus on either facts, specific methods, goals, or values. Frustration and anger can occur when one individual talks about facts while another is eager to discuss methods. The manager, having carefully listened to the discussion, can clarify the nature of the issues so that the discussion can become more productive.

He can recognize and accept the feelings of the individuals involved.   Irrational feelings are generated in a controversy, even though the participants do not always recognize this fact. Each wants to believe that he is examining the problem "objectively." The manager, recognizing and accepting feelings such as fear, jealousy, anger, or anxiety, may make it possible for the participants squarely to face their true feelings. The effective manager does not take a critical attitude toward these feelings by, in effect, saying, "You have no right to feel angry!" Rather, he tries sincerely to communicate his sympathetic feelings.

Ordinarily, we do no real service to people by encouraging a repression of their feelings or by criticizing them for experiencing fear, anger, and so forth. Such criticism—whether implied or expressed openly—may block the search for new ways out of the controversy. There is considerable evidence that when a person feels threatened or under attack, he tends to become more rigid and therefore more defensive about positions to which he has committed himself.

He can indicate who will make the decision being discussed. Sometimes heated disputes go on with respect to issues over which one or more of the persons involved has no control. When people have differing notions about the formal authority available to each, a clarification by the manager of the authority relationships can go far toward placing the discussion in clearer perspective.

He can suggest procedures and ground rules for resolving the differences. If the disagreement is over *facts,* the manager may assist the disputants in validating existing data and in seeking additional data which will more clearly illuminate the issues under dispute.

If the disagreement is over *methods*, the manager may first want to remind the parties that they have common objectives, and that their disagreement is over means rather than ends. He may suggest that before examining in detail each of their proposed methods for achieving the goals, they might together establish a set of criteria to be used in evaluating whatever procedures are proposed. He may also want to suggest that some time be spent in trying to generate additional alternatives reflecting new approaches. Then after these alternatives have been worked out, he may encourage the parties to evaluate them with the aid of the criteria which these persons have developed together.

If the disagreement is over *goals* or goal priorities, he may suggest that the parties take time to describe as clearly as possible the conflicting goals which are being sought. Sometimes arguments persist simply because the parties have not taken the trouble to clarify for themselves and for each other exactly what they do desire. Once these goals are clearly stated, the issues can be dealt with more realistically.

If the disagreement is over *values*, the manager may suggest that these values be described in operational terms. Discussions of abstractions often tend to be fruitless because the same words and concepts mean different things to different people. To help individuals become more fully aware of the limitations to which their actions are subject, the question, "What do you think you can do about this situation?" usually leads to a more productive discussion than the question, "What do you believe in?" Because value systems are so closely related to a person's self concept, the manager may want to give particular attention to protecting the egos involved. He may make clear that an individual's entire ethical system is not being scrutinized, but only those values which are pertinent to the particular instance.

He can give primary attention to maintaining relationships between the disputing parties. Sometimes, during the course of a heated dispute, so much attention is paid to the issue under discussion that nothing is done to maintain and strengthen the relationship between the disputing parties. It is not surprising, therefore, that disputes tend to disrupt ongoing relationships. Through oversight or deliberate action, important functions are neglected which sustain or further develop human relationships—for example, the functions of encouraging, supporting, reducing tension, and expressing common feelings. If a conflict is to be transformed into a problem-solving situation, these functions need to be performed by someone—either by the manager or, through his continuing encouragement, by the parties themselves.

He can create appropriate vehicles for communication among the disputing parties.   One of the ways to bring differences into a problem-solving context is to ensure that the disputants can come together easily. If they can discuss their differences *before* their positions become crystalized, the chances of their learning from each other and arriving at mutually agreeable positions are increased. Having easy access to one another is also a way of reducing the likelihood that each will develop unreal stereotypes of the other.

Misunderstanding mounts as communication becomes more difficult. One of the values of regular staff meetings, therefore, is that such meetings, properly conducted, can provide a continuing opportunity for persons to exchange ideas and feelings.

If the manager wishes his subordinates to deal with their differences in a problem-solving framework, he will want to ask himself, "In what kind of setting will the parties to this dispute be best able to discuss their differences with a minimum of interference and threat?" He will exclude from such a setting any individuals whose presence will embarrass the disputants if the latter "back down" from previously held points of view. It will be a setting which reflects as much informality and psychological comfort as possible.

He can suggest procedures which facilitate problem solving. One of the key needs in a dispute is to separate an idea from the person who first proposes it. This increases the chance of examining the idea critically and objectively without implying criticism of the person. Techniques like brainstorming, for example, are designed to free people from the necessity to defend their ideas during an exploration period. Another facilitating action is outlining an orderly set of procedures (e.g., examining objectives, obtaining relevant data) for the disputants to follow as they seek a constructive resolution of their difference.

Managerial Objectivity

Thus far we have tended to make the unrealistic assumption that the manager is able to maintain his own objectivity in the face of a difference among his subordinates. Obviously, this does not easily happen because his feelings also tend to become involved. It is, in fact, not unusual for people to react to differences more on the basis of their own feelings than on the basis of some rational approach to the problem at hand.

A manager may be deeply concerned about the disruptive effects of a disagreement. He may be troubled about how the persistence of a dispute will affect him personally or his position in the organization. He may worry about the danger of coming under personal attack, or of incurring the anger and hostility of important subordinates or a superior. He may become anxious as another person expresses deep feelings, without really understanding why.

While sometimes personal feelings of this kind are at the conscious level, often they are unrecognized by the manager himself because they lie in the area of the unconscious. This, then, highlights the importance of the manager's own self-awareness. While we do not intend to deal with this topic here, it might be well to note some "alerting signals" to which the manager might pay attention when he confronts a difference.

Certain kinds of behavior may indicate that the manager's handling of differences is strongly influenced by his personal needs and feelings rather than by the objective interests of the organization—as, for example:

- A persistent tendency to surround himself with yes men.

- Emphasizing loyalty and cooperation in a way that makes disagreement seem equivalent to disloyalty and rebellion.

- A persistent tendency to "pour oil on troubled waters" whenever differences arise.

- Glossing over serious differences in order to maintain an appearance of harmony and teamwork.

- Accepting ambiguous resolutions of differences which permit conflicting parties to arrive at dissimilar interpretations.

- Exploiting differences to strengthen his personal position of influence through the weakening of the position of others.

Any of these kinds of behavior could, as we have already suggested, be appropriate in certain situations and actually serve the general interest of the organization. If, however, they represent rather consistent patterns on the part of the manager, then it may be worth his while to examine more closely the reasons for his actions.

There are times in the lives of most of us when our personal needs are the strongest determinants of our behavior. Fortunately, most organizations can tolerate a limited amount of such self-oriented behavior on the part of their managers. The danger occurs if an individual believes that his actions are solely motivated by the "good of the organization" when, in fact, he is operating on the basis of other kinds of personal motivation without being aware of it.

The manager who is more fully aware of his own feelings and inclinations is in a better position to diagnose a situation accurately and to choose rationally the kind of behavior which is in the best interests of the organization.

Conclusion

This article began with the assumption that many managers are uncertain and uneasy when differences arise. Because their own emotions and the feelings of others quickly become involved, they often deal with differences in a haphazard or inappropriate manner. We have attempted to suggest some more systematic ways to view differences and to deal with them. We believe that if a manager can approach a difference with less fear and with greater awareness of the potential richness that lies in it, he will better understand the basic nature and causes of the difference. And having done this, he will be in a better position to discover and implement more realistic alternatives for dealing with it.

Conflict . . .

is a theme that has occupied the thinking of man more than any other, save only God and love. In the vast output of discourse on the subject, conflict has been treated in every conceivable way. It has been treated descriptively, as in history and fiction; it has been treated in an aura of moral approval, as in epos; with implicit resignation, as in tragedy; with moral disapproval, as in pacifistic religions. There is a body of knowledge called military science, presumably concerned with strategies of armed conflict. There are innumerable handbooks, which teach how to play specific games of strategy. Psychoanalysts are investigating the genesis of "fight-like" situations within the individual, and social psychologists are doing the same on the level of groups and social classes. . . .

I suspect that the most important result of a systematic and many-sided study of conflict would be the changes which such a study could effect in ourselves, the conscious and unconscious, the willing and unwilling participants in conflicts. Thus, the rewards to be realistically hoped for are the indirect ones, as was the case with the sons who were told to dig for buried treasure in the vineyard. They found no treasure, but they improved the soil.[3]

Notes

1. For insightful treatments of the causes and consequences of conflict, and the alternative means of dealing with it— as well as with other expressions of difference—see Lewis A. Coser, *The Function of Social Conflict* (London, Routledge and Kegan Paul, Ltd., 1956); and Raymond W. Mack

and Richard C. Snyder, "The Analysis of Social Conflict—Toward an Overview and Synthesis," *Conflict Resolution,* June 1957, pp. 212–248.

2. For definitions and discussions of social sensitivity and action flexibility see Robert Tannenbaum and Fred Massarik, "Leadership: A Frame of Reference," *Management Science,* Vol. 4, No. 1, October 1957; and Robert Tannenbaum and Warren H. Schmidt, "How to Choose a Leadership Pattern," HBR March–April 1958, p. 95.

3. Anatol Rapoport, *Fights, Games, and Debates* (Ann Arbor: The University of Michigan Press, 1960) pp. 11, 360.

Originally published in November–December 1960
Reprint 60612

The Team That Wasn't

SUZY WETLAUFER

Executive Summary

"YOU HAVE ONE RESPONSIBILITY as FireArt's director
of strategy," the CEO had said to Eric on his first day.
"That's to put together a team of our top people, one
from each division, and have a comprehensive plan for
our strategic realignment up, running, and winning within
six months."

It seemed like an exciting, rewarding challenge. The
team approach to problem solving was Eric's specialty;
in his old job, he had managed three teams of manufacturing specialists. Clearly, this project would be difficult:
FireArt was trying to combat an 18-month slump in sales
and earnings. But Eric was sure that together, the glass-
maker's top managers could find a way to reverse the
trend.

Unfortunately, the team got off on the wrong foot
from its first meeting. Randy Louderback, FireArt's

charismatic and extremely talented director of sales and marketing, seemed intent on sabotaging the group's efforts. In fact, at the first three team meetings, Randy either dominated the discussion or withdrew entirely, tapping his pen on the table to indicate his boredom. Sometimes, he withheld information vital to the group's debate, or he denigrated people's comments.

Anxiously awaiting the start of the team's fourth meeting, Eric was determined to address Randy's behavior openly in the group. But before he could, Randy again provoked a confrontation, and the meeting ended abruptly.

What should Eric do now? Is Randy the team's only problem? Seven experts discuss the characters in this fictitious case study and examine what it takes to create a successful team.

T HE LAST THING ERIC HOLT had expected to miss about New York City was its sunrises. Seeing one usually meant he had pulled another all-nighter at the consulting firm where, as a vice president, he had managed three teams of manufacturing specialists. But as he stood on the balcony of his new apartment in the small Indiana city that was now his home, Eric suddenly felt a pang of nostalgia for the way the dawn plays off the skyscrapers of Manhattan. In the next moment, though, he let out a sardonic laugh. The dawn light was *not* what he missed about New York, he realized. What he missed was the feeling of accomplishment that usually accompanied those sunrises.

An all-nighter in New York had meant hours of intense work with a cadre of committed, enthusiastic colleagues. Give and take. Humor. Progress. Here, so far anyway, that was unthinkable. As the director of strategy at FireArt, Inc., a regional glass manufacturer, Eric spent all his time trying to get his new team to make it through a meeting without the tension level becoming unbearable. Six of the top-level managers involved seemed determined to turn the company around, but the seventh seemed equally determined to sabotage the process. Forget camaraderie. There had been three meetings so far, and Eric hadn't even been able to get everyone on the same side of an issue.

Eric stepped inside his apartment and checked the clock: only three more hours before he had to watch as Randy Louderback, FireArt's charismatic director of sales and marketing, either dominated the group's discussion or withdrew entirely, tapping his pen on the table to indicate his boredom. Sometimes he withheld information vital to the group's debate; other times he coolly denigrated people's comments. Still, Eric realized, Randy held the group in such thrall because of his dynamic personality, his almost legendary past, and his close relationship with FireArt's CEO that he could not be ignored. And at least once during each meeting, he offered an insight about the industry or the company that was so perceptive that Eric knew he *shouldn't* be ignored.

As he prepared to leave for the office, Eric felt the familiar frustration that had started building during the team's first meeting a month earlier. It was then that Randy had first insinuated, with what sounded like a joke, that he wasn't cut out to be a team player. "Leaders lead, followers . . . please pipe down!" had been his exact words, although he had smiled winningly as he spoke, and the rest of the group had laughed heartily in response. No one in the group was laughing now, though, least of all Eric.

FireArt, Inc., was in trouble—not deep trouble, but enough for its CEO, Jack Derry, to make strategic repositioning Eric's top and only task. The company, a family-owned maker of wine goblets, beer steins, ashtrays, and other glass novelties had succeeded for nearly 80 years as a high-quality, high-price producer, catering to hundreds of Midwestern clients. It traditionally did big business every football season, selling commemorative knickknacks to the fans of teams such as the Fighting Irish, the Wolverines, and the Golden Gophers. In the spring, there was always a rush of demand for senior prom items—champagne goblets emblazoned with a school's name or beer mugs with a school's crest, for example. Fraternities and sororities were steady customers. Year after year, FireArt showed respectable increases at the top and bottom lines, posting $86 million in revenues and $3 million in earnings three years before Eric arrived.

In the last 18 months, though, sales and earnings had flattened. Jack, a grandnephew of the company's founder, thought he knew what was happening. Until recently, large national glass companies had been able to make money only through mass production. Now, however, thanks to new technologies in the glassmaking industry, those companies could execute short runs profitably. They had begun to enter FireArt's niche, Jack had told Eric, and, with their superior resources, it was just a matter of time before they would own it.

"You have one responsibility as FireArt's new director of strategy," Jack had said to Eric on his first day. "That's to put together a team of our top people, one person from each division, and have a comprehensive plan for the company's strategic realignment up, running, and winning within six months."

Eric had immediately compiled a list of the senior managers from human resources, manufacturing, finance, distribution, design, and marketing, and had set a date for the first meeting. Then, drawing on his years as a consultant who had worked almost solely in team environments, Eric had carefully prepared a structure and guidelines for the group's discussions, disagreements, and decisions, which he planned to propose to the members for their input before they began working together.

Successful groups are part art, part science, Eric knew, but he also believed that with every member's full commitment, a team proved the adage that the whole is greater than the sum of its parts. Knowing that managers at FireArt were unaccustomed to the team process, however, Eric imagined he might get some resistance from one or two members.

For one, he had been worried about Ray LaPierre of manufacturing. Ray was a giant of a man who had run the furnaces for some 35 years, following in his father's footsteps. Although he was a former high school football star who was known among workers in the factory for his hearty laugh and his love

Ironically, the people Eric thought would be problems weren't. Randy was the problem.

of practical jokes, Ray usually didn't say much around FireArt's executives, citing his lack of higher education as the reason. Eric had thought the team atmosphere might intimidate him.

Eric had also anticipated a bit of a fight from Maureen Turner of the design division, who was known to complain that FireArt didn't appreciate its six artists. Eric had expected that Maureen might have a chip on her shoulder about collaborating with people who didn't understand the design process.

Ironically, both those fears had proved groundless, but another, more difficult problem had arisen. The wild card had turned out to be Randy. Eric had met Randy once before the team started its work and had found him to be enormously intelligent, energetic, and good-humored. What's more, Jack Derry had confirmed his impressions, telling him that Randy "had the best mind" at FireArt. It was also from Jack that Eric had first learned of Randy's hardscrabble yet inspirational personal history.

Poor as a child, he had worked as a security guard and short-order cook to put himself through the state college, from which he graduated with top honors. Soon after, he started his own advertising and market research firm in Indianapolis, and within the decade, he had built it into a company employing 50 people to service some of the region's most prestigious accounts. His success brought with it a measure

"If Randy can't help you, no one can," CEO Jack Derry had told Eric.

of fame: articles in the local media, invitations to the statehouse, even an honorary degree from an Indiana business college. But in the late 1980s, Randy's firm suffered the same fate as many other advertising shops, and he was forced to declare bankruptcy. FireArt considered it a coup when it landed him as director of marketing, since he had let it be known that he was offered at least two dozen other jobs. "Randy is the future of this company," Jack Derry had told Eric. "If he can't help you, no one can. I look forward to hearing what a team with his kind of horsepower can come up with to steer us away from the mess we're in."

Those words echoed in Eric's mind as he sat, with increasing anxiety, through the team's first and second meetings. Though Eric had planned an agenda for each meeting and tried to keep the discussions on track, Randy always seemed to find a way to disrupt the process. Time and time again, he shot down other people's ideas, or he simply didn't pay attention. He also answered most questions put to him with maddening vagueness. "I'll have my assistant look into it when he gets a moment," he replied when one team member asked him to list FireArt's five largest customers. "Some days you eat the bear, and other days the bear eats you," he joked another time, when asked why sales to fraternities had recently nose-dived.

Randy's negativism, however, was countered by occasional comments so insightful that they stopped the conversation cold or turned it around entirely—comments that demonstrated extraordinary knowledge about competitors or glass technology or customers' buying patterns. The help wouldn't last, though; Randy would quickly revert to his role as team renegade.

The third meeting, last week, had ended in chaos. Ray LaPierre, Maureen Turner, and the distribution director, Carl Simmons, had each planned to present cost-cutting proposals, and at first it looked as though the group were making good progress.

Ray opened the meeting, proposing a plan for FireArt to cut throughput time by 3% and raw-materials costs by 2%, thereby positioning the company to compete better on price. It was obvious from his detailed presentation that he had put a lot of thought into his comments, and it was evident that he was fighting a certain amount of nervousness as he made them.

"I know I don't have the book smarts of most of you in this room," he had begun, "but here goes anyway." During his presentation, Ray stopped several times to answer questions from the team, and as he went on, his nervousness transformed into his usual ebullience. "That wasn't so bad!" he laughed to himself as he sat down at the end, flashing a grin at Eric. "Maybe we *can* turn this old ship around."

Maureen Turner had followed Ray. While not disagreeing with him—she praised his comments, in fact—she argued that FireArt also needed to invest in new artists, pitching its competitive advantage in better design and wider variety. Unlike Ray, Maureen had made this case to FireArt's top executives many times, only to be rebuffed, and some of her frustration seeped through as she explained her reasoning yet again. At one point, her voice almost broke as she described how hard she had worked in her first ten years at FireArt, hoping that someone in management would recognize the creativity of her designs. "But no one did," she recalled with a sad shake of her head. "That's why when I was made director of the department, I made sure all the artists were respected for what they are—*artists*, not worker ants. There's a difference, you know." However, just as with Ray LaPierre, Maureen's comments lost their defensiveness as the group members, with the exception of Randy, who remained impassive, greeted her words with nods of encouragement.

By the time Carl Simmons of distribution started to speak, the mood in the room was approaching buoyant. Carl, a quiet and meticulous man, jumped from his seat and practically paced the room as he described his ideas. FireArt, he said, should play to its strength as a service-oriented company and restructure its trucking system to increase the speed of delivery. He described how a similar strategy had been adopted with excellent results at his last job at a ceramics plant. Carl had joined FireArt just six months earlier. It was when Carl began to describe those results in detail that Randy brought the meeting to an unpleasant halt by letting out a loud groan. "Let's just do *everything*, why don't we, including redesign the kitchen sink!" he cried with mock enthusiasm. That remark sent Carl back quickly to his seat, where he halfheartedly summed up his comments. A few minutes later, he excused himself, saying he had another meeting. Soon the others made excuses to leave, too, and the room became empty.

No wonder Eric was apprehensive about the fourth meeting. He was therefore surprised when he entered the room and found the whole group, save Randy, already assembled.

Ten minutes passed in awkward small talk, and, looking from face to face, Eric could see his own frustration reflected. He also detected an edge of panic—just what he had hoped to avoid. He decided he had to raise the topic of Randy's attitude openly, but just as he started, Randy ambled into the room, smiling. "Sorry, folks," he said lightly, holding up a cup of coffee as if it were explanation enough for his tardiness.

"Randy, I'm glad you're here," Eric began, "because I think today we should begin by talking about the group itself—"

Randy cut Eric off with a small, sarcastic laugh. "Uh-oh, I knew this was going to happen," he said.

Before Eric could answer, Ray LaPierre stood up and walked over to Randy, bending over to look him in the eye.

"You just don't care, do you?" he began, his voice so angry it startled everyone in the room.

Everyone except Randy. "Quite the contrary—I care very much," he answered breezily. "I just don't believe this is how change should be made. A brilliant idea never came out of a *team*. Brilliant ideas come from brilliant individuals, who then inspire others in the organization to implement them."

"That's a lot of bull," Ray shot back. "You just want all the credit for the success, and you don't want to share it with anyone."

"That's absurd," Randy laughed again. "I'm not trying to impress anyone here at FireArt. I don't need to. I want this company to succeed as much as you do, but I believe, and I believe passionately, that groups are useless. Consensus means mediocrity. I'm sorry, but it does."

"But you haven't even *tried* to reach consensus with us," Maureen interjected. "It's as if you don't care what we all have to say. We can't work alone for a solution—we need to understand each other. Don't you see that?"

The room was silent as Randy shrugged his shoulders noncommittally. He stared at the table, a blank expression on his face.

It was Eric who broke the silence. "Randy, this is a *team*. You are part of it," he said, trying to catch Randy's eye without success. "Perhaps we should start again—"

Randy stopped him by holding up his cup, as if making a toast. "Okay, look, I'll behave from now on," he said. The words held promise, but he was smirking as he spoke them—something no one at the table missed. Eric took a deep breath before he answered; as much as he wanted and needed Randy Louderback's help, he was suddenly struck by the thought that perhaps Randy's personality and his past experiences simply made it impossible for him to participate in the delicate process of ego surrender that any kind of teamwork requires.

"Listen, everyone, I know this is a challenge," Eric began, but he was cut short by Randy's pencil-tapping on the table. A moment later, Ray LaPierre was standing again.

"Forget it. This is never going to work. It's just a waste of time for all of us," he said, more resigned than gruff.

"We're all in this together, or there's no point." He headed for the door, and before Eric could stop him, two others were at his heels.

Why Doesn't This Team Work?

Seven experts discuss what teamwork takes.

JON R. KATZENBACH *is a director of McKinsey & Company and coauthor, with Douglas K. Smith, of* The Wisdom of Teams: Creating the High-Performance Organization *(Harvard Business School Press, 1993; HarperCollins, 1994). Their video,* The Discipline of Teams, *was published by Harvard Business School Management Productions.*

Eric has his hands full with this team, particularly with Randy. In fact, a skeptic might well advise Eric to throw in the towel now because it is clear that Randy can—and might—destroy the team for good. But there are other factors hindering this team besides Randy, and unless Eric recognizes and addresses them, the team will not make progress, whatever its makeup.

There is no evidence of a common commitment to a team purpose or a working approach. Eric is trying valiantly to hold the members to an agenda based on the CEO's charge: "to have a comprehensive plan for strategic realignment." At best, that's a vague directive. Consequently, the members do not understand the implications of those words, draw any meaningful focus from them, or recognize any need to work together to make "strategic realignment" a performance reality.

The "rules of the road" are extremely unclear. While the team has a good mix of skills and experience, the members do not know how each is expected to contribute, how they will work together, what they will work on together, how the meetings will be conducted, or how each person's "nonteam" responsibilities will be handled.

Eric's consultant "team" experience is misleading. In the past, Eric was really a part of a consultant "working group," which is completely different from a team. For one thing, consultants generally have prior experience dealing with the client assignments they obtain. For another, consultant working groups expect to have leaders; they're usually formed with the understanding that one person knows best how to accomplish the task at hand efficiently with minimal risk. Finally, most of the real work in such a group is done by individuals as individuals, not by individuals relying on one another to accomplish joint tasks. I doubt that Eric's experience in New York was at all similar to the situation that confronts him at FireArt, yet he seems to expect this "team" to gel and operate in a similar fashion.

Eric's group spends more time on feelings and past experiences than on the task at hand. We know little about what they are supposed to be working on and accomplishing. Except for Randy, the members are supportive and helpful—to the point where protecting feelings becomes more important than getting something done. Real teams do not have to get along. They have to get things accomplished.

Eric's group seeks consensus rather than accomplishment. Real teams seldom seek consensus; they decide each issue differently based on who is in the best position to ensure performance. Sometimes the leader decides, sometimes another person, and sometimes more than one. Consensus may happen now and then, but it is not the litmus test for a team's performance.

So what can be done? First, Eric must acknowledge that most would-be teams go through a painful metamorphosis; his group is not uncommon. Having said that, though, he must also recognize that not every group of multiskilled, well-intended people can or should function as a team. In this case, the likelihood of team performance is hard to determine because it has not yet been fully tested. Before giving up on the idea, therefore, Eric can try several things—provided he can also enlist the support of the team's sponsor (CEO Jack Derry) in these attempts.

First, he can decide whether these people should make up a leader-driven "working group" rather than a "team." Is this really a team-performance opportunity? If so, it should be evident that the multiple, diverse skills of the members will make a material difference in the results of their efforts. It

If Randy will not follow the rules, either the team or Randy must go.

must become evident to all members that no one person "knows best"—not even Randy. If the members are to work primarily on individual subassignments and report back to the group, and if the "sum of the individual bests" is good enough, then Eric does not need a team. If it is truly a team opportunity, Eric and/or Jack should:

1. Insist that the team identify specific work "products" that require several members to work together. The value of these products must be significant relative to the group's overall performance, and Randy must recognize both the value and the need for collective work and

skills. If this can be accomplished, the team members can be expected to develop trust and respect by working together to those ends, regardless of personal chemistries and past attitudes.

2. Require the team members to determine how to hold themselves mutually accountable for achieving their goals. Teams need mutual or joint accountability in addition to individual accountability. The entire group must believe it can succeed or fail only as a team.

3. Design a more disciplined working approach that enforces "team basics." It should ensure that members do as much real work in team (or subteam) settings as they do separately in preparing for the team sessions. A member giving presentations to the rest of the team seldom constitutes collective work for purposes of increasing team performance. Eric should also set clear and enforceable ground rules to which all members must abide. If Randy still will not follow the rules, either the team or Randy must go. Some people cannot be team members.

The "Randy issue" must be addressed. I suspect Eric has been too quick to assume the worst. Randy may or may not be a team misfit. After all, he has had little chance so far to change his attitude about this team. His bravado tells us only what he thinks of teams in general; many excellent team members begin with this attitude. The only way to find out if this team can include Randy is for him to do real work with other members individually to see if mutual trust and respect develop.

If all else fails, Eric should consider a dual or split working approach that does not include Randy in many of the important working meetings. Otherwise, this "team" may do its best as a leader-driven working group, with Eric playing a stronger leader role. They are not all that bad!

J. RICHARD HACKMAN *is the Cahners-Rabb Professor of Social and Organizational Psychology at Harvard University in Cambridge, Massachusetts. He holds appointments both in the psychology department and at the Harvard Business School. His most recent book,* Groups That Work (And Those That Don't) *was published in 1990 by Jossey-Bass.*

Some people aren't cut out to be team players. Eric should have paid attention when Randy suggested that he was one of those people.

Eric could have met with Randy privately after that meeting. The first order of business would have been for Eric to assure himself that Randy indeed felt unable to work on a team—and that his self-perception was grounded in reality. That established, the two managers could then have sought a way to capture Randy's insights that did not require him to be a regular team member. Who knows what they might have come up with? Perhaps Eric would meet privately with Randy before and after each team meeting to report progress and seek ideas. Perhaps such briefings would be done by different team members in rotation. Perhaps Randy would be invited to certain meetings, or portions of them, but only when his ideas or reactions were especially needed.

Every organization has some members who make their best contributions as solo performers. These are people who just don't have the skills needed to work constructively in teams—and who are unable or unwilling to acquire those skills. Such people are found in all functions and at all levels, even in senior management. There are only three ways to deal with them when teams are formed. One, keep them at a safe distance from the teams so they can do no damage. (Some companies these days seek to get rid of their solo performers altogether: "Only team players at this company!" is the slogan. As if being a team player were the ultimate measure of anyone's worth, which it is not.) Two, go ahead and put them on teams, install strong leaders to keep things under control, and hope for the best. ("Everybody here works on teams. No exceptions!" is the motto then. As if all people were skilled in teamwork, which they are not.)

Neither of these alternatives has much to recommend it. The first is wasteful. Talent is knowingly withheld from teams. The second is dangerous. Team after team can be sunk by "team destroyers" like Randy—people whose brilliance in individual tasks is matched by their incapacity for collaborative work. (Less talented individuals are less of a problem. If they persist in misbehaving, the team can afford to get rid of them. But it is very hard even to contemplate shunning someone as good as Randy.)

The only realistic alternative, then, is to harvest the contributions of talented people like Randy in a way that does not put the team itself at risk. As I said, Eric should have sought a way to accomplish that immediately after the first meeting. His goal now should be the same. It will be harder now than it would have been then because now he also has considerable repair work to do with Randy and with the team. The task also requires greater care now than it would have then because of the risk of scapegoating.

Teams that encounter frustrating problems as they are working sometimes attach to a single team member all the negative feelings that are rampant in the group. They make that person the scapegoat, the one who is responsible for everything that has gone wrong. If that bad actor could just be removed, the thinking goes, the team's problems would disappear. The impulse to scapegoat someone when the going gets rough can be quite strong; moreover, the scapegoated member often starts to behave in accordance with his or her peers' expectations, which makes things worse all around. Therefore, teams must not too quickly blame any one person for in-process problems. Midcourse corrections in team composition can be accomplished, but they are risky and difficult. It is better to get team composition right when the team is formed than to undertake repair work later.

When reviewing how well a team is doing, I ask three questions. First, does the product or service of the team meet the standards of its clients—those who receive, review, or use the team's work? Second, is the team becoming more capable as a performing unit over time? Third, does membership on the team contribute positively to each person's learning and well-being? Despite an excellent launch, FireArt's strategic repositioning team is now failing on all three criteria.

Eric should once again review the team's direction, its structure, and his own leadership. Such matters should always be considered first, before attributing team problems to the attitudes or skills of individual members. But if Eric finds, as I suspect he will, that the basic performance situation of this team is actually quite favorable, then he will have to confront Randy's apparent incapacity for teamwork directly. Not to do so would be an abdication of his responsibility as team leader.

GENEVIÈVE SEGOL *is a principal scientist in the research and development department at Bechtel Corporation in San Francisco, California.*

People work well as a team, but they don't think well as a team. That is the essence of what Randy is saying in his arrogant way: "A brilliant idea never came out of a team. Brilliant ideas come from brilliant individuals, who then inspire others in the organization to implement them." From this standpoint, Randy is right. The team assembled by Eric would not succeed even if Randy were not bent on sabotaging the process, because its objective is too vague and its leadership is too weak.

The team was given the task of developing a plan for strategic realignment and having it implemented within six months. This guideline is totally insufficient, especially because the members of the team are unaccustomed to working together and probably uncomfortable with conceptual discussions. They are confused by the mandate, and, as a result, they are shooting in all directions. Worse, they do not realize (or want to admit) that they do not understand the issue. No one has asked the basic question: What is the real problem with FireArt's business?

Jack Derry, the CEO, "thought" the company's faltering financial results were caused by the entry of large glassmaking companies into its niche market, but that analysis is superficial. Are customers going to competitors because they offer lower prices, a broader selection, or better service? The solutions proposed by the managers of manufacturing, design, and distribution indicate that each has a different answer to this question. Someone must define the primary cause of FireArt's declining market share and direct the team to focus on that specific issue. That is the first step toward solving the problem presented in this case.

This team would not succeed even if Randy were cooperating. Its objective is too vague, and its leadership too weak.

Defining the problem and giving precise directions to the team should have been the responsibility of FireArt's senior management, but clearly the leadership is lacking. The CEO's hands-off attitude is inappropriate, especially considering that the company's future is at stake. Not only did he fail to anticipate and avoid the present downturn, but when the troubles became apparent, he hired an outsider to correct the situation. The CEO is content to "look forward to hearing what [this] team...can come up with to steer us away from the mess we're in."

This is not delegation but abdication. Unfortunately, Eric has not so far filled that leadership void. Instead, he has played his prepared script, focusing on the mechanics of the teamwork process and hoping for harmony. He certainly did not control the meetings, and Randy took advantage of his timidity. To his credit, however, Eric has already acknowledged that Randy should not be ignored. He must be kept on the team because he has valuable information and insight, and also because he can do more damage to the team if he is not on it. Keeping Randy involved is the second important step.

Eric can simultaneously address the two key issues—giving the team precise directives and keeping Randy involved—by assigning to the latter the responsibility of researching and documenting the exact nature of FireArt's difficulties. Randy will appreciate this individual task; he's also uniquely qualified for the job because of both his intellect and his position. As director of sales and marketing, he is the closest to customers and competitors, and the data must come from them. What's more, this type of assignment is quite analytical and, for this reason, performed more effectively by one person than by a group.

Purists might argue that permitting one individual to be in the spotlight compromises the team's process, but that is nonsense. Teamwork is a business expedient, not a philosophy, and rules may be bent when necessary. Randy will report his findings to the team, and this event should be used by Eric to relaunch the group's effort on a solid basis, that is, with a precise objective—for example, to cut costs by 10% or to be able to fill any order within ten days. Eric must also arrange for the CEO to attend the meeting at which Randy will make his presentation, and a few subsequent team meetings as well, both to control Randy, who is unlikely to be obnoxious in the presence of his boss, and to impress on the group the urgency and importance of its effort.

Eric must act fast, not only because the necessary turnaround of the business cannot wait but also because there is another wild card: Randy might quit. He is an opportunist and an entrepreneur, has little allegiance to FireArt, and enjoys a legendary reputation in the industry, where he has many connections. Eric's job will only be harder if Randy moves to a competitor's team.

PAUL P. BAARD *is an associate professor of communications and management at Fordham University's Graduate School of Business in New York City, with a principal research interest in motivation. He is a former senior corporate executive, and consults with organizations concerning interpersonal issues.*

The truth is, Randy cannot destroy this team unless the other members enable him to do so. Right now, however, an enormous amount of work energy is being lost to reading between the lines, overreacting to perceived slights, pursuing reassurance, and competing instead of cooperating. The group is in danger.

The problem is psychological fusion—a disorder that is running amok in today's stressed corporate environment. In essence, fusion is the failure of one person to separate himself or herself from the words or actions of another. Fusion occurs when we fail to differentiate ourselves emotionally from the opinions and conduct of others. When we allow other people to "make us feel" either good or bad—as a result of compliments or criticism—we have fused with them. Randy was able to drive team members from the room not because he had authority but because they fused with him. These grown adults allowed Randy to make them feel inadequate. They acted as if they *needed* Randy's approval of their ideas. Eric appears to think that he *needs* Randy on the team, which renders Eric unable to interact effectively with him.

The problem is psychological fusion—a disorder that is rampant in corporations today.

Randy, for his part, is caught up in fusion. He clings to the myth that because he is the brightest he is the most effective, and he must have this affirmed continuously by his colleagues. This leaves him unable to acknowledge and support others' good ideas; he is threatened when others have answers too.

Ironically, fusion leads to distance—either overt, as in walking away, or covert, as in withdrawing from a discussion. Because fusion creates pain (from feeling emotionally dependent on others), it leaves people anxious about what others are thinking, saying, and meaning by their words, looks, and even their silences. An individual afflicted with fusion takes on a desperate tone and will usually defend his or her ideas in an emotional way:

"That's my baby you're attacking!" Fusion thus inhibits cooperation and understanding, which are essential to a group's productivity.

The condition of the group is not irreversible, however. There are several things Eric can do to turn the situation around. To begin, he must confront Randy with reality in a private conversation.

Eric must make it clear that FireArt needs a new direction and that Eric's group *will recommend* that path. He should tell Randy that his input is indeed desired. But Eric must also tell Randy that if he is to be a member of the team, he must now play a full role. He is to contribute, challenge, and support ideas as appropriate. And he must clarify and take responsibility for

The situation in the team is not irreversible. Eric can do several things to turn it around. He must confront Randy with reality.

his positions. By being sarcastic, Randy may be offering a comment, but he is not taking a stance. We don't know, for example, what specifically about the other team members' proposals Randy doesn't like; we just know he doesn't like them.

Eric must also let Randy know that it's an all-or-nothing proposition. Eric must ask him, "Will you function in the way I have just described?" An affirmative response is usually forthcoming from malcontents who are confronted this way. If the answer is "no," however, Eric must accept Randy's resignation from the group. And he must not worry about Randy's relationship with the CEO. Unless Jack calls him on his actions, Eric has a right and a responsibility to run the group in the way he believes will yield the best results. (If Jack does call Eric on his actions, Eric will have reason on his side. Jack may think Randy is terrific, but he hired Eric to turn the company around.)

After Eric and Randy meet, Eric should turn his attention to damage control with the rest of the group. To get past the recent strain among the members, Eric should start the next meeting, with everyone present, by stating that Randy had not understood his job in the group—namely to help develop a new strategy for the company, but that now he does. Eric should then explain that each member is responsible for taking a position on all matters, sharing and either defending it or modifying it in discussions or debates.

As the team moves forward, Eric ought to expect that Randy will resort at times to his old ways—using sarcasm or tapping his pencil. If he does, Eric should confront Randy immediately with: "Randy, you and I agreed you would make your position clear. I cannot discern your position based on the comment (or gesture) you just made. What are your thoughts on this matter?"

Right now, psychological fusion has created a tense, threatening environment for all members of this team. But over time, they should be able to develop a healthier expectation of appropriate conduct within the group. This, in turn, will support Randy's improved behavior. When fusion has been removed, Randy's only ability to influence the other members will be the strength of his ideas—a scenario that he and the other group members will find much more satisfying and conducive to a creative process.

ED MUSSELWHITE *is the president and chief executive officer of Zenger-Miller, Inc., a San Jose–based international strategic consulting and business training company.* KATHLEEN HURSON *is the senior vice*

president of research and development at Zenger-Miller.
They are the coauthors, with John H. Zenger and Craig
Perrin, of Leading Teams: Mastering the New Role *(Irwin*
Professional Publishing, 1993). Musselwhite is also a
coauthor, with Jack Orsburn, Linda Moran, and John H.
Zenger, of Self-Directed Work Teams: The New Ameri-
can Challenge *(Irwin Professional Publishing, 1990).*

Can this team be saved? Maybe. The key will be Eric's
ability to focus his unruly team members not on the
team itself but on an inspiring goal that only the team
can achieve. And the task is enormously important. The
success of the organization may hinge on the success of
this team.

For many people contemplating teams, this case
represents their darkest nightmare: the brilliant loner
refusing to cooperate, the other members goaded into
personal attack, the leader powerless to control the
situation, and the hoped-
for progress dashed. In
our experience, few team
members behave so outra-
geously. What's more
common—and more insidious—is that some people's
concerns go underground, where they harden into resistance and outright sabotage. In fact, in a 1994 independent Zenger-Miller survey conducted by the American
Institutes for Research, more than one-third of the
1,000-plus respondent organizations reported that
strong internal resistance and/or sabotage is a significant barrier to be overcome on the road to successful
team implementations.

Some people's concerns
may harden into resistance
and outright sabotage.

This case confirms our belief that shortchanging a
team launch—especially an executive team launch—is

always a mistake. Eric's guidelines for group debate do not begin to cover the orientation, skills training, and goal setting that an effective team launch must contain. We suspect that Eric gave in to deadline pressure and a fear that executive team members would not stand for any touchy-feely stuff. Nevertheless, we have found that executives must receive careful training if they are to function as effective members of a team (as opposed to a traditional executive committee). By and large, these are men and women whose individually focused competitiveness and ability to advance the interests of their own departments have gotten them where they are. The team format represents a radical departure from the environs in which they have previously excelled.

By skipping the critical team-launch process, Eric has gotten himself into a classic team-leadership pickle. To renew trust and foster cohesiveness, he probably should open things up through a series of team meetings in which a progress check is made, mistakes are admitted (including his own), everyone's reactions and feelings are elicited, and agreement is reached on next steps. However, in order to reach the CEO's six-month goal for the company, we recommend that Eric take a few immediate shortcuts.

First, he should have a serious talk with Jack, the CEO. Eric needs to make it clear that without more involvement from Jack, this team is history, and Eric will be headed back to those Manhattan sunrises he misses so much. Having captured Jack's attention, Eric needs to spell out what Jack, and only Jack, can do: provide a lot more visible and behind-the-scenes support for team activities *and* neutralize Randy. Jack's message to Randy should be: (1) this company can't succeed without you; (2) the team is a fact of life; and (3) you don't have to be on it, but you can't sabotage it, either. (At the same time, Jack must be careful not to give other team members the idea that membership is elective.)

Although it's tempting to try to turn Randy into a team player, we think the team stands a better chance of reaching its goal if Eric doesn't focus too much on that one problem. Thus far, Randy has chosen to bring along antiteam baggage. Instead of forcing that issue prematurely—which could trigger Randy's untimely resignation—Eric first should try to create a useful and compatible role for Randy as a special consultant to the team, called in for review or advice whenever the team needs his expertise. As he begins to see the team's successes and feels more and more cut off from its decisions and camaraderie, Randy may eventually want to get more involved. He should be encouraged to do so, although we don't think he will ever be a consummate team player. Not everyone is.

With Randy neutralized for a bit, Eric's next challenges will be to get himself and his team trained and to help the team members create a compelling and results-oriented realignment strategy. The problems facing this organization cry out for effective cross-functional team solutions and innovations.

Instead of the uninspiring department-focused improvements presented by Maureen, Ray, and Carl, we'd like to see the team trained to take a bigger-picture, cross-departmental approach to its realignment task. Working to create cross-functional improvements will jar the executives out of their departmental allegiances and give them a much-needed companywide perspective.

What are the key strategic processes that cut across all departments? How do they affect customers? How should they? Where are the opportunities for improvement? For example, how can Maureen's artists and Ray's furnace workers get together to cut costs, streamline processes, and create new and better products? How can manufacturing and distribution cooperate to make delivery speed a real competitive advantage? High-level cross-functional teams such as this one can meaningfully explore these kinds of questions. And the answers usually produce the biggest organizational improvements.

MICHAEL GARBER *is the manager of quality and employee involvement and training at USG Corporation in Chicago, Illinois.*

Eric is not leading a team. He is facilitating a meeting of a group of individuals who don't really understand the concepts, methods, or importance of teamwork—individuals who are each lobbying for their own personal goals. In fact, it's somewhat surprising that the CEO, Jack Derry, decided to solve FireArt's problems with a team in the first place. The company clearly operates with a traditional, hierarchical management structure, not a structure that supports teamwork.

Teamwork does not occur simply by mandate from above. Nor does it occur overnight. It requires a supportive corporate culture, certain management and interpersonal skills, and practice. Eric has none of these at his disposal except his own experience, so in a sense he must start from scratch at FireArt. I suggest the following action plan:

First, Jack Derry must visit the team to champion its efforts. He must also request periodic updates from the team. His doing that will link the team to the organization and show the group that the company is genuinely interested in and supports its efforts.

Then, Ray, Maureen, et al., need to learn more about the concepts behind teamwork and the benefits of working on a team. They need to know what's in it for them as well as what's in it for the organization. They should hear about successful team efforts in other companies and be educated about common obstacles teams face and specific tools that can help build consensus. To accomplish this, Eric might consider holding an on-site workshop (run by Eric or by an outsider with expertise) that features discussions about the theory behind team management, a review of current literature on the subject, and simulations of various team situations.

The team members must come to understand that teams, by definition, don't require members to surrender their individuality. Rather, teams work best when members respect one another and believe that each is unique and has something important to add. Therefore, the workshop should also include time to evaluate and improve the members' interpersonal skills—skills such as listening, communicating, and giving and receiving feedback. Of course, most members of the FireArt team would probably argue (as most people do) that they already know how to listen and communicate. But the fact is, when Ray LaPierre says something, Maureen Turner has to do more than nod supportively. She must understand his most important points, grasp their implications, and perhaps even formulate a rebuttal. This is a skill, and it can be taught.

With the workshop complete, the team should focus on developing a mission statement. This is necessary to provide the group with a common purpose, and it should help reduce individual lobbying efforts. Once a mission statement is formed, specific goals can be determined to narrow the team's focus of activity. Each member will then better understand his or her role, and real progress can begin.

Randy is a difficult character, mainly because the CEO has put him on a pedestal—a fact that he is exploiting. But with a new foundation in place, Eric will have increased leverage with Randy because he, along with the other members, will recognize the importance of team-work and be more supportive of it. Together, then, they will be able to begin the process of developing a strategic plan to attack the deteriorating business situation.

Originally published in November–December 1994
Reprint 94612

HBR's cases are derived from the experiences of real companies and real people. As written, they are hypothetical, and the names used are fictitious.

Overcoming Group Warfare

ROBERT R. BLAKE AND JANE S. MOUTON

Executive Summary

THE COMPANY YOU RUN stands on the threshold of success. The competition's new product has serious flaws, and all you need do to take giant strides toward controlling market share is to hit the market with your new product. Nothing stands in your way except, of course, that pesky misunderstanding between the product design group and manufacturing. They just can't seem to get along, and it does look as if you may have to push the start-up date back a little. You realize suddenly that if the battle between the two groups doesn't end, the product may not get to market in time to take advantage of the space your competitor has left.

What should you do? The authors of this article present two very different approaches to resolving conflicts between embattled groups. In one method, a neutral facilitator tries to mediate between the two groups by offering compromises and trying to get each group to see the other's point of view. In the other method, the groups form their own views of what their ideal relationship should be and a neutral administrator helps them go though steps to achieve it. Examining two cases of conflict in detail, the authors show how the two approaches work, discuss the outsider's role in each, and offer guidelines for deciding when one approach is likely to work better than the other.

W HILE MANY PEOPLE WORRIED about the absence of experienced air traffic controllers after the Professional Air Traffic Controllers Organization went on strike in 1981, they also wondered why it was so difficult for the FAA and PATCO to come to terms before the strike was called. Important groups that need to cooperate can often overcome their difficulties and continue working together, but sometimes they can't. Over the years disputants in the transportation and coal industries have had skirmishes that have resulted in open warfare. Even when the battles are not waged so publicly or fiercely, the human and material costs organizations pay can be staggering.

We have identified two strategies for resolving intergroup conflicts, each with variations. What we have come to call the *interpersonal facilitator approach* relies on a neutral person to provide a bridge to help disputing parties find common ground. The facilitator does this by identifying areas of agreement as well as disagreement so that the latter can be reduced and resolution achieved.

In what we call the *interface conflict-solving approach,* disputants deal with each other directly as members of whole groups. A neutral person helps the groups go through a program of steps that aids principal members of both groups to identify and resolve their differences.

Line managers and internal consultants who are respected and neutral may serve as facilitators or administrators of the step program. The person selected should be of a rank comparable to or higher than that of the highest-ranking member in either of the groups in conflict. A neutral of lesser rank is likely to be brushed aside by a higher-ranking member in a group bent on attack. When the conflict is between headquarters and a subsidiary or when top management is involved in both groups, as in a merger, the groups should consider calling in an outsider who will have no stake in the outcome.

In the first approach, the facilitator on occasion becomes involved in the discussions themselves and carries messages and proposals from one side to the other. In the second approach, the spokesperson or administrator is uninvolved in the content of discussions and acts principally as a guide to the process.

These two models are quite different, and any reader who wishes to use one or the other approach needs to understand their pros and cons. In what follows, we present two actual but disguised cases that illuminate the benefits and pitfalls of the two models and show how each works. The first case involves a long-term conflict between central engineering and plant management in a large industrial complex. The second case is a union-management conflict of long standing.

Trouble at the Elco Corporation

In this description of how the interpersonal facilitator approach worked at the Elco Corporation, we present the events chronologically through a month of negotiations.

THE STORY AND THE PLAYERS

The president of Elco, Stewart McFadden, had been frustrated for a long time by reports of constant bickering and poor cooperation between central engineering and plant management. Among the many things McFadden told Jim Craig when hiring him as vice president of human resources, was, "This is a nasty situation. I'd like you to take a look at it."

About a month later, when it came up again, Craig said to the president, "I've met several people from both central engineering and plant management, and it looks like quite a one-sided problem to me. The people in central engineering aren't involved that much. They feel this problem is one of those inevitable tensions in organization life, and they are trying to be patient. But the people in plant management are up in arms. They are furious."

"It's hopeless," said McFadden.

"That depends," said Craig, "on whether the problem is one of competence or of communication. If it's the former, yes, it's hopeless. If it's the latter, it's not."

"Competence? No way. They are the cream of the crop—upper 10% of graduating classes, all of them. So it's not competence. Can you help?" McFadden asked.

"Well, I've been through a lot of hang points with unions, and in principle this situation is no different. They realize I'm a newcomer with no ax to grind. Possibly I can get them together to talk it out. At least it's worth a try."

"Anything," said McFadden. "I'm so sick of it. What do you propose?"

"I'd like to get the principals of both groups together for a day or two to get the facts out on the table. Then we'll see what can be done," said Craig.

"You've got my blessing. I look forward to whatever

happens, even if you have to bang a few heads together to get their attention."

Later that week, Craig, Walt Reeves, vice president of engineering, and Jack Lewis, central coordinator of the plant management group, set up the meetings. They agreed that the purpose of the meetings was to study how the groups might cooperate. Reeves wanted Craig to take part in any negotiations as a full partner, speaking for Elco headquarters, and Lewis wanted Craig to mediate the discussions but not to formulate and present substantive proposals.

By offering the services of his office, Craig made it appropriate that he implement his own strategy. He planned for the two groups to meet initially as one large group. Craig saw himself as a facilitator. "My thought was," he reported later, "that both groups would come to know and understand each other better in a constructive atmosphere and that they would trust me to be honest and fair in my role as moderator, mediator, and, if necessary, active negotiator. I also thought that without an established agenda, the main issues would surface."

Accompanying Walt Reeves from central engineering were four of his key personnel. With Jack Lewis from the plant management group were five others—two from the plant in question and three from different plants. Craig himself was joined by other senior personnel, including the human resources advisors assigned to central engineering and to plant management. From time to time, depending on the issue, the group consulted other senior people.

MUTUAL TRUST AND RESPECT

The first meeting was held in a large room that didn't have a table. To break up a "we-they" seating arrangement and help each person participate according to his or her own convictions rather than follow a party line, Craig placed the chairs at spaced intervals around the room.

Craig, seated near the center, opened the meeting. "As you know, the president has long been concerned about how to get your groups to cooperate. He asked me to see if I could help. This meeting has no agenda beyond what the problem is and how we can solve it. Anyone is free to speak, but to keep things moving forward, I will moderate the discussion. Who'd like to start?"

"I'll tell you the problem," a member from central engineering said. "Each engineering discipline, not to mention emerging new materials and construction techniques, is becoming more complex. Plus we've got rapid changes in requirements from EPA, the Nuclear Regulatory Commission, OSHA, and half a dozen other agencies. The heavy fines for operations that violate requirements are bound to teach us all a lesson we should have learned long ago. On these scores, we've got to keep ourselves risk free. There's no option but to centralize engineering."

"That's not the problem at all," a member of plant management shot back. "We're qualified engineers, every one of us, but we are treated like children who can't be trusted to build a derrick with an erector set. It's demeaning. We manage millions in operating expenses, but we can't spend $100 on an air conditioning duct."

The meeting thereupon broke down into mutual recriminations. Later, trying a new tack, Craig stopped trying to moderate discussion between the two groups and held meetings with the two leaders instead.

From the very beginning, Craig had felt that Walt Reeves and Jack Lewis didn't trust or respect each other, and he thought that if he could get them into an informal setting, things would ease between them. He thought it was important for Reeves and Lewis to know each other better before he brought the two groups together again.

Craig wanted to accentuate the positive. He cautioned Lewis not to overreact when he first heard Reeves's formal statement about central engineering being responsible for 100% of engineering and plant management for 100% of operations.

After the first meeting between Reeves and Lewis, Craig reported that "the meeting did produce a buildup of tensions. Reeves's fixed position in regard to the 100% engineering concept was the primary reason. I already knew this to be entirely unacceptable to Lewis. We didn't make much progress, and another session was scheduled."

At this point Craig was not free to reveal to Lewis what Reeves had told him in confidence. Later Craig said, "I felt Reeves was ready to make immediate, even if minor, modifications," such as recommending an increase in the amount plant managers could authorize for small projects. Craig also knew that Reeves deeply distrusted Lewis's reasons for wanting to do "gut" engineering. He tried to help Reeves appreciate Lewis's motives.

Craig used the same strategy again and again: "When we got under way, I stepped back from the discussions because I wanted them to speak to each other directly. Soon they refrained from talking to me or even attempting to draw me into the conversation. Their talk was full of accusations and counteraccusations. Their faces became flushed. The niceties of diplomatic protocol slipped away. They had almost forgotten I was there, while I just continued taking notes.

"Eventually, the argument bogged down when each began to repeat himself and to ignore the other. By the end they were both talking at once. My attempts to change the subject were futile. As they moved toward the door, I got in front of them to block the way. I urged them not to stop these conversations but to give me another chance to use my influence. I said, 'If you have no confidence in me, then these tensions will remain.'

"Lewis agreed readily. I looked Reeves in the eye, and finally he nodded agreement. They left without speaking to each other. During the 30 or so days this effort took, I spent a lot of time preventing the sessions from being interrupted or terminated and in defending and explaining each of them to the other."

During the next few meetings, Craig took a more active role: "I began acting as a referee and made efforts to put the discussion back on track, occasionally explaining what I thought someone meant when the other person seemed to misinterpret it. After one of these sessions, when they were going back to their offices, Reeves drew me aside and said, 'Look, I don't want to talk to that SOB anymore. If you want to talk to him, you can represent my point of view, but I've had it up to here. Tell me about any progress you make, and I promise to be as constructive as possible in meeting their criticisms of us. I want you to understand the issue is not one of simply dividing engineering up in a 25-75 or a 50-50 way. Just to give them *some* will not solve the problem.'"

With this breakdown, it was no longer possible to bring the two men together to discuss their fixed positions. Craig summarized his feelings at the time this way: "I did not know where to go from there. We had accomplished little, except to name the difficult issues and to recognize the depth of disagreements. There was little or no commonality between them as men, and almost every discussion deteriorated into an unproductive argument that reopened old wounds. The final meeting ended with Reeves and Lewis casting accusations at each other."

Craig now shifted to the go-between strategy, which became the arrangement for the remainder of the month. He proposed that he be an intermediary who formulated positions. "I asked them to give me the opportunity to devise my own compromise proposals and to present my views to both of them."

As he continued to work with various individuals and subgroups within both departments, Craig drafted proposals. Then he met again with each principal to solicit reactions to his ideas. He expressed his intention to each as follows: "This proposal is drafted with the idea that neither side will alter it substantially. I've tried to keep in mind what your group wants and needs. My commitment is to continue to try to represent your interests and to negotiate for you."

BETTER TIMES

The turning point in Reeves's attitude came after he and Craig had slipped into a win-lose argument about the necessity for central engineering to accept some local engineering on small-plant projects. The hot, unpleasant, and repetitive argument deteriorated until Craig stood up to leave and accused Reeves of being willing to give up peace with plant management because of an unrealistic, rigid position. Craig explained what had happened: "My strong statement made me appear tilted to the plant's perspective and therefore less trustworthy.

"In a final effort to persuade Reeves to continue these negotiations," Craig continued, "I explained the serious consequences of unilaterally breaking off. This action would harm the relationship between central engineering, the personnel function, and the corporate offices. He would be violating his promises to me, and the onus of failure would be on him. Also, I described how headquarters might give up and simply realign assignments by edict."

Reeves saw the seriousness of the situation and realized that even though he wasn't convinced about Lewis's motives or whether concessions would satisfy him, he would have to be less rigid himself.

Ultimately, the relationship between Reeves and Lewis improved, but the division of responsibility for engineering and operations did not change. Three central engineering people now provide liaison engineering. They are located so that they can quickly communicate and troubleshoot as well as provide the plant employees firsthand knowledge of in-plant engineering activities. The liaisons have reduced tensions and improved services in a variety of ways—removing bottlenecks, solving priority issues, and enabling engineering to do more realistic, functional design work. A gray area that allows plant managers to do a few functions in the name of maintenance, which in fact do involve some engineering, now exists between construction and maintenance.

WHAT CRAIG DID

Jim Craig's role during the negotiations shifted often. When pushed to the wall, for instance, on occasion Craig himself would become confrontational. He too became angry and fearful of disastrous consequences if something didn't change. But he kept discussion moving with many intervention techniques:

Building anticipation. Before the meetings Craig told Lewis that Reeves was coming forward with the strongest statement about a 100% to a 0% engineering-operations proposal and the reasons why. He also reported to Reeves that Lewis had no plans beyond trying to work with the situation as it developed.

Controlling discussion. When the going got tough, Craig authorized who should speak to whom and in what order, particularly in the three-way discussions: "I asked Reeves to begin—I then asked Lewis to respond—" and so forth.

Reversing antagonists' roles. Craig helped each participant clarify his understanding of the other's position by asking, "Would you repeat what Reeves just said?" and asking for confirmation: "Is that a fair statement?"

Relieving tension. After Reeves's strong initial presentation, Craig ended the strained silence by saying, "Perhaps it's appropriate now for Jack to accept the position as stated and send a memo around to that effect."

Transmitting information. Craig passed information between the two principals to prevent the process from breaking down: "I conveyed Lewis's position to Reeves by saying, 'Lewis sincerely wants to continue to explore how to make use of plant engineers to do local engineering.'"

Formulating proposals. From the beginning, Craig saw part of his job as drafting possible solutions and proposing them to the principals.

Near the end of the process, as he shuttled back and forth, Craig kept coming up with new ideas. He suggested that central engineering perform a check-and-balance function when the people in the plants did some engineering on their own. Although things do not always run smoothly at Elco, enough of the conflict has been resolved that the disagreements between engineering and plant management are not constant thorns in McFadden's side. Jim Craig continues to shuttle, keeping sparks from becoming fires.

The Hillside Strike

Another, though less familiar, approach also works effectively in dealing with conflict between groups. Underlying this approach is the assumption that key leaders and their staffs in whole groups can resolve win-lose conflicts through direct confrontation.

The Hillside facility, a large modern plant serving the paper products industry, was wracked by an unresolved management-union conflict. Like true enemies, both parties had placed themselves in peril to deprive the other of a "victory."

After months of conflict, Jeff O'Hare, plant manager, said, "We are on a collision course toward a contract expiration date only months away. If a positive, productive relationship can't be established, it means another head-on clash. I'm not sure how we'd survive another shutdown as a viable economic entity, but I am sure that when and if we start up again, this plant won't be operated by the same people who are managing and operating it now."

RELATIONSHIP-BUILDING STRATEGY

Hal Floyd, corporate employee relations manager, proposed to Jeff O'Hare that they try solving their problems with the union face to face. Floyd had read about a situation similar to Hillside's in which a union and management had used the interface approach. O'Hare reluctantly agreed.

Floyd explored the possibility with the president of the local union, Rick Keenan, and then both made a joint pitch to the international union representative, Bruce Boyd. Boyd was as pessimistic and doubtful as O'Hare had been but agreed, saying, "I don't want to be accused of causing a strike because I wouldn't respond to a constructive gesture." Since no one in the company or the union could be regarded as neutral, Floyd contracted with an outsider to act as administrator.

Six members of top management and six union officials made up the two groups participating in the meetings. Because its members sat together, each group kept its feeling of solidarity. The administrator, Bob, started the sessions by reviewing goals.

"Our goal for this session is to answer the question, Can these two groups shift from a destructive relationship based on fear and suspicion to a problem-solving relationship based on respect?"

Bob explained the procedure: "As a first step, each group is to meet separately to prepare descriptions of what a sound union-management relationship would be for Hillside. You should record these on large sheets so that we can compare them at a joint session. Each group should select a spokesperson to present its conclusions in the next general session. The spokesperson may be the designated leader, but since O'Hare and Keenan have faced one another so many times in the past, it may be better to ask someone else to give your reports.

"The rest of you should try to avoid taking spontaneous potshots. They don't produce useful insights and often just cause counterattacks, which only make things worse. If you feel something important needs to be said, ask the spokesperson if you may speak. After you finish, you'll identify the similarities and differences in your separately produced descriptions to develop a consolidated model to which both groups can be committed."

He continued: "The next step is to describe the actual conditions that characterize the here and now. You'll later consolidate these into a joint statement of union-management problems at Hillside. You can then identify steps you can take to move away from the antagonistic situation to a cooperative one, with specific plans for follow-up, review, and reevaluation.

"To keep track of what's going on," he said, "I'll be in and out of both rooms, but I don't expect to take an active part. I'll be happy to answer any questions about the procedure."

VISUALIZING A SOUND RELATIONSHIP

At first, management seemed unable to concentrate on trying to formulate the ideal sound relationship. The session began with O'Hare questioning Keenan's, the union president's, motivations.

"I wonder what Keenan means by 'recognition'?" said O'Hare, referring to a remark Keenan had made in the joint meeting.

"Special treatment for the union president is my guess," Mike Barret, general foreman, replied. "We know they want to run the plant."

"Give 'em an inch," Allen, head of maintenance, commented supportively, "I've seen it over and over—they'll squeeze this plant dry, even dryer than it already is."

"I can't respect Keenan or his tactics," Sam Kobel, the manufacturing supervisor, said. "Maybe we'd be better off with somebody else as union president. He's a political animal. He doesn't care about the plant or the people. He just wants to move up the union ladder."

Management knew that Keenan wielded considerable influence over the membership. Wayne, the personnel manager, said, "When he personally favors a management proposal, he presents it at the union hall in a straightforward, positive way. If he wants a proposal rejected, he twists it to emphasize negative implications and works to see it defeated."

After venting their anger, which often participants must do before they can take a more constructive approach, management concentrated on identifying the elements of a sound relationship: mutual trust, honesty, effective communication, problem solving, and consistency. The union also started on a negative note before producing its list, which was similar to management's.

Walking toward the general session room, O'Hare overheard Melton, the shop steward, muttering to Keenan, "We'll see this kind of relationship with those buzzards when hell freezes over." Keenan nodded to the apparent truth in Melton's remark.

O'Hare shot back, "It wouldn't take long for us to agree on that, would it?" Bob, the administrator, noted this exchange but said nothing since it was not a part of the formal meetings.

When they convened in a general session to exchange their separately developed statements, the spokespersons chosen by each group made their presentations and questioned one another's meaning. The ideal relationship each proposed seemed so remote from actuality that neither the union nor management viewed it as realistic. Before sending them off to separate meeting places, Bob asked the two groups to rate each statement in the other's report on a four-point scale:

1. "We agree with the statement as written."

2. "We agree with the statement as rewritten in the following way."

3. "We wish to ask the following questions for further clarification."

4. "We disagree with the statement for the following reasons."

He stated that each group could ask the other's spokesperson to explain the numbers and reasons for the ratings. As the two groups converted the 4's, 3's, and 2's into 1's, reflecting mutual agreement, the statements became part of the consolidated ideal model.

GETTING DOWN TO BRASS TACKS

The next step in the process is for each group to describe as objectively as possible the present reality. The members of the groups should explore specific factors that have shaped and influenced the relationship as well as the barriers that have stifled progress. At Hillside, management and the union were so preoccupied with the details of recent conflict and perceived injustice that they were anxious to begin describing actual conditions—where the real battleground was.

From management's perspective, the union was usurping authority and responsibility, thereby justifying to management its distrust and disrespect.

The union maintained that while it did not want to "run" the plant, it had much to contribute to productivity and efficiency but would withhold effort until members were treated with dignity and respect. The exhibit, "Perceptions of Actual Relationship at Hillside," shows how management and the union viewed the situation.

When each side revealed its view of the situation, both parties seemed stunned at the depth of the cleavage and each other's unhappiness. Recognizing that both groups had agreed to the properties of a sound relationship, management was particularly shaken by the union's conviction that, given prevailing attitudes and behavior, progress was impossible. With the plant's future on the line, along with their careers, the top managers could not reconcile themselves to giving up.

At this point each group was asked to return to its team room to digest the implications of the other's input and to apply the four-point method to the other's perception of the situation.

THE TIPOVER

The first shift in position occurred when management began comparing the two descriptions of the actual relationship, particularly the two views of "cooperation," and saw how far apart they were.

"How could two groups work in the same plant, grappling with the same problems, and see each other with such diametrically opposed viewpoints?" O'Hare asked the management group. "What do they mean, 'Cooperation is one-sided—it means doing what the company says'? During the past ten years we've given away more valuable clauses in the name of cooperation and lost

Perceptions of Actual Relationship at Hillside

Management's View	Union's View	Consolidated View
We have an adversary relationship. It's we versus they.	Hopelessness; a shutdown is necessary to bring them to their senses. We're ready for the shutdown.	Our adversary relationship promotes readiness for win–lose clashes; a strike is preferable to perpetual humiliation.
There's mistrust on both sides. Cooperation means consenting to union demands. The union wants comanagement.	Cooperation is one-sided: it means doing what the company says. Hopelessness extends to all workers. Dignity is lost in a guard-prisoner relationship.	Mistrust prevails; cooperation is misinterpreted by the company as compliance and by the union as the company conceding to union demands.
The union does not give its members a true picture of management's position. Cooperation is lacking in the promotion of efficiency and economy. Use outsiders to resolve internal issues.	Management cares only for production; people be damned. Management destroys people's incentive.	Without measuring the consequences, management concentrates on production, and the union conveys this attitude to its members.
Management acknowledges low credibility with union members; the union president has low credibility with management.	Management blames past regimes for problems; it sees no deficiency in itself. This plant is our home for life but management's hotel until the next round of promotions.	Leaders have not earned credibility from one another; they do not make the relationship viable as a long-term investment.
Management is only enforcing existing rules and agreement interpretation but is seen by the union as inflexible and enforcing the contract to the hilt in order to be provocative.	The union can't get its foot in the door to solve the problems.	The union accepts the exercise of initiative as a management prerogative, but management sees the union's offers of help through informal testing before decisions are finalized as comanagement.

more management prerogatives than any other plant in our area of competition."

"As far as I can see," said Kobel, manufacturing supervisor, "when you say 'given away,' literally that is what it's been. We've given away paragraph after paragraph and have gotten nothing in return."

"You can say that again," piped up Allen, maintenance director. "I'm so fed up with some people sitting on their fannies waiting for other people to work. If one could give a helping hand to the other, they could get the job done in half the time. We keep falling further behind."

"I propose," said Bruce Wayne, the personnel manager, "that we give this item a 4. We just flatly disagree with it."

"Hold it, fellas," said Mike Barret. "Let's look at what's been going on in the past few weeks and see how these guys could say such a thing. Any of you heard them say things in meetings you've had with them?"

"Well," said Wayne, "they think we're trying to erode the contract. They think we're putting unreasonable interpretations on various clauses and challenging them to file grievances, to which we say, 'Arbitrate.' They say this is our search-and-destroy technique."

As they continued, discussion kept returning to the first item on the union's list, "hopelessness." The contradiction between what management expected—that is, "militancy"—and what it observed—"despair and hopelessness"—compelled management to reexamine in a candid way how it could have the expectations it did.

"Does Keenan really speak for the membership when he says a strike is inevitable," O'Hare asked, "or is he just trying to shake us up?"

"It doesn't matter," Floyd said. "If he wants a strike, he can convince the people."

"And," said Mike Barret, "they know it."

"What are you hearing," questioned O'Hare, "when you talk outside the plant? Is there talk in the community about a strike? Are spouses unhappy?"

"Keenan has the strike vote in his pocket as far as I can tell," Wayne said. "He can get them riled up. If he doesn't have complete support now, he will by May. He and his cronies can convince the rest that a strike will ultimately be to their advantage. Make no mistake, he's a strong leader."

Surprised by Wayne's report of the union's reaction to what it called "unreasonable interpretations that pushed members to file grievances," O'Hare said, "Maybe we'd better look at ourselves more objectively before pointing any more fingers at them. How have you seen me relating to Keenan and the others?" he asked.

"I see you coming across as strong and hard-nosed," Allen said.

"I think you're open, forthright, and honest to the point of being naive," Floyd observed. "You've had a good reputation as a production and people man. Lately, though, I've seen you change to using force—no discussion, no alternatives, no involvement, pure force."

Wayne added, "In the past I've seen you as open, honest, fair. You listen well and take good advice. But I think you're shifting toward a tough attitude."

"I haven't seen much of a change since you've been here," Barret said. "It seems you've always been direct and aggressive."

Kobel spoke last. "I don't have much to add," he said. "Basically, I agree with what's been said. O'Hare is fair, but firm—to the point of being stubborn, I guess."

Having heard the others, O'Hare summed up his own feelings. "You're right," he said. "I think I'm so determined to turn this thing around, I've become unreasonable. It's much easier to blame our problems on my predecessors or to dump them on Keenan and his cohorts. I thought I'd kept a pretty open mind, but if my attitudes seem rigid to you, they probably seem even more so to them."

The management group then examined each member's attitude toward the union in turn. While individual differences were present, the management team shared similar attitudes, and each recognized how destructive his own actions had become. Allen ended the discussion by saying, "It's clear that we're the ones who are going to have to change."

"It won't be easy," Barret said.

"We've described the kind of relationship we want in the ideal," O'Hare said. "Now we need to decide how to get there."

"Look at what we've done in the past few months," Allen remarked. "We've created the image that we're only out for production—that we care nothing for people. They say we've destroyed the incentive for people to make any input at all."

O'Hare responded, "We don't have any choice but to try for the best relationship we can."

"I feel that's an important first step," Floyd commented. "It isn't going to be easy to turn around years of antagonism, frustration, and disappointment, and your recognition of the hard work involved is a positive sign."

"What about the rest of you?" O'Hare asked. "What do you think?"

"What other option do we have?" Kobel responded, and the others nodded affirmatively.

"What should we do now—communicate our feelings to the union?" asked Allen.

"What else is there to do?" O'Hare said.

"Okay, then, let's prepare a summary of our quandary and present it," Barret suggested.

Management made a list of five statements describing its thoughts and feelings at the time. While management grappled with its own contribution to the current conflict, the union members collected evidence of management's refusal to deal constructively.

"It's no use trying to help," they concluded. "Management sees only what it wants to, and it wants to see us as responsible for all its problems and failures. What it never seems to realize is that for management Hillside is an assignment. Two, three, or four years and they're gone. For us, it's a lifetime. Do we want a plant that's not a profit maker? Nothing could be dumber. But we're not twentieth-century slaves either. We can't work overtime just to cover up their goof-offs. We can go the last mile, but to go beyond destroys our self-respect."

After each group had had the opportunity to formulate a response to the other's assessment of the actual relationship, the two groups met again to share their reactions.

CONVERGENCE OF CONVICTIONS

O'Hare went to Bob and said, "Look, I want to speak my own feelings, which the others agree to. Don't worry about my polarizing it."

Bob started the session by saying, "O'Hare has asked to begin by telling about management's self-study description."

O'Hare introduced the group's self-study by saying, "I guess we were concerned and angry with you in the beginning. There was a lot of blaming and finger pointing until we began really to look at ourselves." He then presented the five items shown in the exhibit "Hillside Management's Description of Its Thoughts and Feelings."

"I'd like your reactions," O'Hare said.

"Speaking for the union," Boyd, the international union representative, replied, "this comes as a total surprise, given the way things have been building up. We're really pleased that you're willing to take these steps. Both sides stand to benefit. We don't want a caucus, but we do want to go back and talk a moment among ourselves."

Leaving the room, Melton commented to Keenan, "I never believed it was possible."

O'Hare, who overheard the remark, said, "I suppose this means 'hell has frozen over'?"

"No," said Keenan, "it doesn't mean that at all."

Hillside Management's Description of Its Thoughts and Feelings

1	We recognize that we have a deep win–lose orientation toward the union.
2	We want to change!
3	We have challenges to meet: to convince the union we want to change, to convince ourselves we have the patience and skill and conviction to change.
4	We're responsible for bringing the rest of management on board.
5	We recognize the risk but want to resist the temptation to revert to a win–lose stance when things get tough.

When the groups reconvened, Melton spoke for the union: "Our reaction is that your self-study is a giant step. We recognize it must have been hard for you to face up to the need for such drastic change. We can't tell you how welcome it is. We'll cooperate in any way to bring about the change."

Because both management and the union saw the possibility of pursuing a shared goal, each contributing from the standpoint of what was in the best interest of the plant, the tension underlying the relationship broke. This positive attitude led to a desire to get to specifics. Once the two groups gave up their antagonistic stance, they found that agreement was possible in areas where they had been deadlocked for months. For instance, at one point in the discussion of certain problems, O'Hare and Keenan were looking together at the 77 grievances that had been filed. Keenan commented, "I'm sure we've filed a number of grievances more for their annoyance value than for the merit of the issues involved."

O'Hare quickly responded, "And we've dillydallied in answering them and have opted for no action whenever it was legally reasonable to do so."

"We can withdraw those that have annoyance value only, identify the real issues, and clear up the situation," Keenan said.

"You won't get a no from me on that," O'Hare responded.

SMOOTH SAILING

Several years have passed since the day O'Hare and Keenan sat down together to look at the list of grievances. How has the plant changed since the union-management meeting? In the final step of the program, ten union-management task forces grappled with problems or groups of problems. Each brought proposed solutions to the plant manager, who considered the recommendations and either approved or modified them or provided a full and satisfactory explanation for why he could not. The union has not called a strike during this time, and both union and management judge this plant to be tops in problem solving. Before the union and management got together, the plant was eleventh in the financial performance of the company's plants; today it is number one.

BOB'S ROLE

The administrator of this five-step program makes many contributions to ensure that the interface conflict-solving approach is effective. This person:

Sets expectations. Bob described the objectives and activities involved in each step of the program.

Establishes ground rules for the general sessions. Bob made sure, for instance, that up to the point where tempers quieted only the spokespersons for each group were to speak.

Determines sequence. Bob established which spokesperson would speak first. This arrangement is preferable to group members volunteering to speak first.

Monitors for candor. The design administrator monitors teams to ensure openness on a within-group basis.

Curbs open expression of hostile attitudes between groups. Bob intervened to let participants who made snide remarks know that they were breaking the ground rules.

Avoids evaluation. Bob didn't evaluate the progress or quality of group efforts, nor did he respond to inquiries regarding content or the issues being discussed.

Introduces procedures to reduce disagreements.
When the group reached an impasse, Bob suggested procedures for breaking the deadlock, such as the four-point rating method.

Ensures understanding. When each spokesperson had finished speaking, Bob made sure that the other spokesperson had no further questions and that answers were to the point.

Follows up. After the meetings, Bob helped set follow-up schedules to ensure that the changes were implemented.

Which Model Should You Use?

The interpersonal facilitator model has many adherents. The concept is inherent in the idea of the honest broker and is present when a lawyer seeks an out-of-court settlement between conflicting parties. In each case the objective is to create a meeting of minds without dictating the terms or the outcome.

In our experience, however, the prospect of success in relieving tensions between adversary groups is much greater when managers use the interface conflict-solving approach rather than the interpersonal facilitator model. While the latter has become a more or less standard approach, it has severe limitations.

In the exhibit, "Comparison of Two Approaches to Intergroup Problem Solving," we compare the two models in regard to some important factors such as who should comprise the groups and what the expert's role is.

The exhibit, "When to Use Each Model," offers guidelines for judging which approach stands the greatest likelihood of resolving conflicts between opposing parties that impede organizational success.

The facilitator approach tends to be most successful when the outcome produced constitutes a compromise of differences and is a mutually acceptable solution to both parties, neither side feeling it has won or lost. But when membership of two or more groups is involved, that kind of compromise is hard to achieve.

Part of the power of the interface conflict-solving approach comes from the participants' lifting their thinking above the status quo to envision a model of a sound relationship. Doing so, they see the relationship in a different light and recognize the possibility of creating a new relationship rather than merely diminishing the negative aspects of the present one.

A second strength of the problem-solving approach is that it forces members of the same group to confront each other. At Hillside, Wayne challenged O'Hare to look at how management had come to use the contract as a weapon rather than as guidance for cooperation.

The reader may well ask, "Why are participants prepared to risk exposure by being open with each other, particularly when they may place themselves in jeopardy?" In many organizations, smoothly operating interfaces, say between management and the union, are crucial. When the pain it suffers from the frustration of being unable to get the job done is greater than the pain it associates with frankness, then management brings itself to the level of candor essential for focusing on the real issues.

Comparison of Two Approaches to Intergroup Problem Solving

Issue	Interpersonal Facilitator Model	Interface Conflict-Solving Model
Composition	Nominal group attendance but top leaders "lead"; top leaders only	Top group plus representatives of major other constituencies who need to be involved
Contact between groups	Primarily with or through facilitator	Through spokespersons in general sessions with group integrity maintained
Facilitator or administrator to deal with	Leaders (and others) usually on a one-to-one basis	All as members of whole groups
Meetings	Exchange of entry positions Formulation of proposals and counterproposals on a one-to-one basis by facilitator or intermediary	Monitoring and validation of design integrity Ideal and actual relationship modeling on an element-by-element basis; consolidation through the four points
Communication between groups or individuals	Message-passing through facilitator Exchange of written positions Proposals made by facilitator	Exchanges through spokespersons, not necessarily leaders, both oral and written
Initial agenda	Perceived tensions and antagonisms	Thinking through the elements of an ideal sound relationship
Role of expert	Go-between Message carrier Spokesperson for other group Solution proposer	Procedural design administrator Not a spokesperson for other group No content role Not a solution proposer
Tactics for dealing with an impasse	Exerting influence on members of group one to one, starting with easiest to persuade Use of acceptance and rejection to induce movement Fear-provoking remarks	Direct interchanges through spokespersons
Time required	Three days to one week (often longer)	Four to five days; follow-up usually months later

Another compelling motivation is the rationality of problem solving. When people see something that is faulty, they want to set it right. The program of steps focuses attention on the contradictions between the sound solution and existing arrangements. When all those who feel a sense of responsibility for solving the

When to Use Each Model

Use the interpersonal facilitator model when:	Use the interface conflict-solving model when:
Only two people are involved.	Support of group members will strengthen implementation of any change.
Personal chemistry blocks direct discussion between the principals.	Personal chemistry problems are not sufficient to prevent participation.
The leader's agreeing to change has no adverse consequences for his or her acceptability as a leader.	The leader's agreeing to change places his or her leadership in jeopardy with those who are being led.
The leaders know the depth and scope of the problem.	The leaders do not know the depth and scope of the problem.
The change can be implemented on the basis of compliance or without agreement about its soundness.	The change can best be implemented by agreement and understanding of its soundness.
A deadline is near and decisions, even though imperfect, are necessary to prevent a total breakdown.	Sufficient time is available to develop basic solutions.
A multiplicity of views exists in both groups and therefore there is no common point of view or shared feeling.	The interface problem is deeply embedded in the culture of both groups.

problem see that both parties agree about what the relationship should be, they share a desire to see the problem solved.

Any executive who is involved in a conflict between groups or who is responsible for groups in dispute should seriously consider which of these two models would work in given situations. The more central and serious the issue is to the relationship between the groups, the greater the likelihood of success using the interface conflict-solving approach has. If the issue is not crucial or serious, the greater the likelihood that it can be resolved through third-party facilitation.

Beyond that, managers can always apply the facilitator model should the conflict-solving model fail, but the reverse is less likely to be true. If the facilitator approach fails, key leaders are not likely to want to try another approach, whereas if the conflict-solving model should fail, the leaders themselves may be ready to continue to seek agreement with the help of a facilitator.

Originally published in November–December 1984
Reprint 84603

This article is adapted from the authors' book, Solving Costly Organizational Conflicts: Achieving Intergroup Trust, Cooperation, and Teamwork *(Jossey-Bass, 1984).*

Negotiating with a Customer You Can't Afford to Lose

THOMAS C. KEISER

Executive Summary

WHEN A CUSTOMER YOU COUNT ON turns combative, your choices are limited. You can't afford to lose the business, but you can't afford to lose the profit either. Confrontation will poison the water, but compromise will rob you of your margin.

The solution to the impasse is to dodge the bullets and lure your customer into a search for inventive answers to tough problems. The author has eight suggestions:

1. Increase your variables and know your walkaway. Price is not the only flexible factor. Consider every aspect of the deal—R&D, specifications, delivery and payment arrangements. The more options you have, the greater your chances of success.

2. When attacked, listen. Keep aggressive customers talking and you will learn valuable things about their business and their needs.

3. To reduce frustration and assure customers that you're hearing what they're saying, pause often to summarize your progress.

4. Assert your own company's needs. Too much empathy for the customer can reduce the emphasis on problem solving and lead to concessions.

5. Try to make your customer commit to the outcome of the whole negotiation. Make sure the full solution works for both parties.

6. Save the hardest issues for last.

7. Start high, concede slowly, keep your expectations high, and remember that every concession has a different value for buyer and seller.

8. Never give in to emotional blackmail. If customers lose their temper, don't lose yours. Withdraw, postpone, dodge, sidestep, listen. As a last resort, declare the attack unacceptable but always refuse to fight.

"I LIKE YOUR PRODUCT, but your price is way out of line. We're used to paying half that much!"

"Acme's going to throw in the service contract for nothing. If you can't match that, you're not even in the running."

"Frankly, I think we've worked out a pretty good deal here, but now you've got to meet my boss. If you thought I was tough . . ."

"Tell you what: If you can drop the price by 20%, I'll give you the business. Once you're in our division, you know, you'll have a lock on the whole company. The volume will be huge!"

"I can't even talk to you about payment schedule. Company policy is ironclad on that point."

"Look here, at *that* price, you're just wasting my time! I thought this was a serious bid! Who do you think you're talking to, some green kid?"

This wasn't supposed to happen. You've invested a lot of time earning a customer's trust and goodwill. You've done needs-satisfaction selling, relationship selling, consultative selling, customer-oriented selling; you've been persuasive and good-humored. But as you approach the close, your good friend the customer suddenly turns into Attila the Hun, demanding a better deal, eager to plunder your company's margin and ride away with the profits. You're left with a lousy choice: do the business unprofitably or don't do the business at all.

This kind of dilemma is nothing new, of course. Deals fall through every day. But businesses that depend on long-term customer relationships have a particular need to avoid win-lose situations, since backing out of a bad deal can cost a lot of future deals as well. Some buyers resort to hardball tactics even when the salesperson has done a consummate job of selling. The premise is that it costs nothing to ask for a concession. Sellers can always say no. They will still do the deal. But many sellers—especially inexperienced ones—say yes to even the most outrageous customer demands. Shrewd buyers can lure even seasoned salespeople into deals based on emotion rather than on solid business sense. So how do you protect your own interests, save the sale, and preserve the relationship when the customer is trying to eat your lunch?

Joining battle is not the solution unless you're the only source of whatever the customer needs. (And in that case you'd better be sure you never lose your monopoly.) Leaving the field is an even worse tactic, however tempting it is to walk away from a really unreasonable customer.

Surprisingly, accommodation and compromise are not the answers either. Often a 10% price discount will make a trivial difference in the commission, so the salesperson quickly concedes it. But besides reducing your company's margin significantly, this kind of easy accommodation encourages the customer to expect something for nothing in future negotiations.

Compromise—splitting the difference, meeting the customer halfway—may save time, but because it fails to meet the needs of either party fully it is not the proverbial win-win solution. A competitor who finds a creative way to satisfy both parties can steal the business.

The best response to aggressive but important customers is a kind of assertive pacifism. Refuse to fight, but refuse to let the customer take advantage of you. Don't cave in, just don't counterattack. Duck, dodge, parry, but hold your ground. Never close a door; keep opening new ones. Try to draw the customer into a creative partnership where the two of you work together for inventive solutions that never occurred to any of your competitors.

There are eight key strategies for moving a customer out of a hardball mentality and into a more productive frame of mind.

1 *Prepare by knowing your walkaway and by building the number of variables you can work with during the negotiation.* Everyone agrees about the walkaway. Whether you're negotiating an arms deal with the Russians, a labor agreement with the UAW, or a contract you can't afford to lose, you need to have a walkaway: a combination of price, terms, and deliverables that represents the least you will accept. Without one, you have no negotiating road map.

Increasing the number of variables is even more important. The more variables you have to work with, the more options you have to offer; the greater your options, the better your chances of closing the deal. With an important customer, your first priority is to avoid take-it-or-leave-it situations and keep the negotiation going long enough to find a workable deal. Too many salespeople think their only variable is price, but such narrow thinking can be the kiss of death. After all, price is one area where the customer's and the supplier's interests are bound to be at odds. Focusing on price can only increase animosity, reduce margin, or both.

Instead, focus on variables where the customer's interests and your own have more in common. For example, a salesperson for a consumer-goods manufacturer might talk to the retailer about more effective ways to use advertising dollars—the retailer's as well as the manufacturer's—to promote the product. By including marketing programs in the discussion, the salesperson helps to build value into the price, which will come up later in the negotiation.

The salesperson's job is to find the specific package of products and services that most effectively increases value for the customer without sacrificing the seller's profit. For example, an automotive parts supplier built up its research and development capacity, giving customers the choice of doing their own R&D in-house or farming it out to the parts supplier. Having this option enabled the supplier to redirect negotiations away from price and toward creation of value in the product-development process. Its revenues and margins improved significantly.

Even with undifferentiated products, you can increase variables by focusing on services. A commodity chemicals salesperson, for example, routinely considered payment options, quantity discounts, bundling with other purchases, even the relative costs and benefits of using the supplier's tank cars or the customer's. Regardless of industry, the more variables you have, the greater your chances of success.

2 *When under attack, listen.* Collect as much information as possible from the customer. Once customers have locked into a position, it is difficult to move them with arguments, however brilliant. Under these circumstances, persuasion is more a function of listening.

Here's an example from my own company. During a protracted negotiation for a large training and development contract, the customer kept trying to drive down the per diem price of our professional seminar leaders. He pleaded poverty, cheaper competition, and company policy. The contract was a big one, but we were already operating at near capacity, so we had little incentive to shave the per diem even slightly. However, we were also selling books to each seminar participant, and that business was at least as important to us as the services. The customer was not asking for concessions on books. He was only thinking of the per diem, and he was beginning to dig in his heels.

At this point our salesperson stopped talking, except to ask questions, and began listening. She learned a great deal—and uncovered an issue more important to the customer than price.

The customer was director of T&D for a large corporation and a man with career ambitions. To get the promotion he wanted, he needed visibility with his superiors. He was afraid that our professionals would develop their own relationships with his company's top management, leaving him out of the loop. Our salesperson decided to give him the control he wanted. Normally we would have hired freelancers to fill the gap between our own available staff and the customer's needs. But in this case she told him he could hire the freelancers himself, subject to our training and direction. The people we already employed would be billed at their full per diem. He would save money on the freelancers he paid directly, without our margin. We would still make our profit on the books and the professional services we did provide. He would maintain control.

Moreover, we were confident that the customer was underestimating the difficulty of hiring, training, and managing freelancers. We took the risk that somewhere down the road the customer would value this service and be willing to pay for it. Our judgment turned out to be accurate. Within a year we had obtained the entire professional services contract without sacrificing margin.

It was a solution no competitor could match because no competitor had listened carefully enough to the customer's underlying agenda. Even more important, the buyer's wary gamesmanship turned to trust, and that trust shaped all our subsequent negotiations.

When under attack, most people's natural response is to defend themselves or to counterattack. For a salesperson in a negotiation, either of these will fuel an upward spiral of heated disagreement. (See "Two Common Mistakes" at the end of this aritcle.) The best response, however counterintuitive, is to keep the customer talking, and for three good reasons. First, new information can increase the room for movement and the number of variables. Second, listening without defending helps to defuse any anger. Third, if you're listening, you're not making concessions.

3 *Keep track of the issues requiring discussion.* Negotiations can get confusing. Customers often get frustrated by an apparent lack of progress; they occasionally go back on agreements already made; they sometimes raise new issues at the last moment. One good way to avoid these problems is to summarize what's already been accomplished and sketch out what still needs to be discussed. Brief but frequent recaps actually help maintain momentum, and they reassure customers that you're listening to their arguments.

The best negotiators can neutralize even the most outspoken opposition by converting objections into issues that need to be addressed. The trick is to keep your cool, pay attention to the customer's words and tone, and wait patiently for a calm moment to summarize your progress.

4 *Assert your company's needs.* Effective salespeople always focus on their customers' interests—not their own. They learn to take on a customer perspective so completely that they project an uncanny understanding of the buyer's needs and wants. Too much empathy can work against salespeople, however, because sales bargaining requires a dual focus—on the customer and on the best interests of one's own company. The best negotiating stance is not a single-minded emphasis on customer satisfaction but a concentration on problem solving that seeks to satisfy both parties. Salespeople who fail to assert the needs of their own company are too likely to make unnecessary concessions.

The style of assertion is also extremely important. It must be nonprovocative. "You use our service center 50% more than our average customer. We've got to be paid for that. . ." will probably spark a defensive reaction from a combative customer. Instead, the salesperson should build common ground by emphasizing shared interests, avoiding inflammatory language, and encouraging discussion of disputed issues. This is a better approach: "It's clear that the service center is a critical piece of the overall package. Right now you're using it 50% more than our average customer, and that's driving up our costs and your price. Let's find a different way of working together to keep service costs down and still keep service quality high. To begin with, let's figure out what's behind these high service demands."

5 *Commit to a solution only after it's certain to work for both parties.* If a competitive customer senses that the salesperson is digging into a position, the chances of successfully closing the deal are dramatically reduced. A better approach is to suggest hypothetical solutions. Compare these two approaches in selling a commercial loan.

"I'll tell you what. If you give us all of the currency exchange business for your European branches, we'll cap this loan at prime plus one."

"You mentioned the currency exchange activity that comes out of your European branches. Suppose you placed that entirely with us. We may be able to give you a break in the pricing of the new loan."

The first is likely to draw a counterproposal from a competitive customer. It keeps the two of you on opposite sides of the negotiating table. The second invites the customer to help shape the proposal. Customers who participate in the search for solutions are much more likely to wind up with a deal they like.

Some salespeople make the mistake of agreeing definitely to an issue without making sure the overall deal still makes sense. This plays into the hands of an aggressive customer trying to get the whole loaf one slice at a time. It's difficult to take back a concession. Instead, wrap up issues tentatively. "We agree to do X, provided we can come up with a suitable agreement on Y and Z."

6 *Save the hardest issues for last.* When you have a lot of points to negotiate, don't start with the toughest, even though it may seem logical to begin with the deal killers. After all, why spend time on side issues without knowing whether the thorniest questions can be resolved?

There are two reasons. First, resolving relatively easy issues creates momentum. Suppose you're working with a customer who's bound and determined to skin you alive when it comes to the main event. By starting with lesser contests and finding inventive solutions, you may get the customer to see the value of exploring new approaches. Second, discussing easier issues may uncover additional variables. These will be helpful when you finally get down to the heart of the negotiation.

7 *Start high and concede slowly.* Competitive customers want to see a return on their negotiation investment. When you know that a customer wants to barter, start off with something you can afford to lose. Obviously, game playing has its price. Not only do you train your customers to ask for concessions, you also teach them never to relax their guard on money matters. Still, when the customer really wants to wheel and deal, you have little choice.

The customer too can pay a price for playing games. A classic case involves a customer who always bragged about his poker winnings, presumably to intimidate salespeople before negotiations got started. "I always leave the table a winner," he seemed to be saying. "Say your prayers." What salespeople actually did was raise their prices 10% to 15% before sitting down to negotiate.

They'd let him win a few dollars, praise his skill, then walk away with the order at a reasonable margin.

A number of studies have shown that high expectations produce the best negotiating results and low expectations the poorest. This is why salespeople must not let themselves be intimidated by the customer who always bargains every point. Once they lower their expectations, they have made the first concession in their own minds before the negotiation gets under way. The customer then gets to take these premature concessions along with the normal allotment to follow.

A man I used to know—the CEO of a company selling software to pharmacies—always insisted on absolute candor in all customer dealings. He'd begin negotiations by showing customers his price list and saying, "Here's our standard price list. But since you're a big chain, we'll give you a discount." He broke the ice with a concession no one had asked for and got his clock cleaned nearly every time.

The key is always to get something in return for concessions and to know their economic value. Remember that any concession is likely to have a different value for buyer and seller, so begin by giving things that the customer values highly but that have little incremental cost for your company:

Control of the process

Assurance of quality

Convenience

Preferred treatment in times of product scarcity

Information on new technology (for example, sharing R&D)

Credit

Timing of delivery

Customization

Service

There's an old saying, "He who concedes first, loses." This may be true in a hardball negotiation where the customer has no other potential source of supply. But in most competitive sales situations, the salesperson has to make the first concession in order to keep the deal alive. Concede in small increments, get something in return, and know the concession's value to both sides. Taking time may seem crazy to salespeople who have learned that time is money. But in a negotiation, not taking time is money.

8 *Don't be trapped by emotional blackmail.* Buyers sometimes use emotion—usually anger—to rattle salespeople into making concessions they wouldn't otherwise make. Some use anger as a premeditated tactic; others are really angry. It doesn't matter whether the emotion is genuine or counterfeit. What does matter is how salespeople react. How do you deal with a customer's rage and manage your own emotions at the same time?

Here are three different techniques that salespeople find useful in handling a customer who uses anger—wittingly or unwittingly—as a manipulative tactic.

- Withdraw. Ask for a recess, consult with the boss, or reschedule the meeting. A change in time and place can change the entire landscape of a negotiation.

- Listen silently while the customer rants and raves. Don't nod your head or say "uh-huh." Maintain eye contact and a neutral expression, but do not reinforce the customer's behavior. When the tirade is over, suggest a constructive agenda.

- React openly to the customer's anger, say that you find it unproductive, and suggest focusing on a specific, nonemotional issue. There are two keys to this technique. The first is timing: don't rush the process or you risk backing the customer into a corner from which there is no graceful escape. The second is to insist that the use of manipulative tactics is unacceptable and then to suggest a constructive agenda. Don't be timid. The only way to pull this off is to be strong and assertive.

For example, imagine this response to a customer throwing a fit: "This attack is not constructive. [Strong eye contact, assertive tone.] We've spent three hours working the issues and trying to arrive at a fair and reasonable solution. Now I suggest that we go back to the question of payment terms and see if we can finalize those."

Of course, there is substantial risk in using any of these techniques. If you withdraw, you may not get a second chance. If you listen silently or react ineffectively, you may alienate the customer further. These are techniques to resort to only when the discussion is in danger of going off the deep end, but at such moments they have saved many a negotiation that looked hopeless.

The essence of negotiating effectively with aggressive customers is to sidestep their attacks and convince them that a common effort at problem solving will be more profitable and productive. Your toughest customers will stop throwing punches if they never connect. Your most difficult buyer will brighten if you can make the process interesting and rewarding. The old toe-to-toe scuffle had its points, no doubt. Trading blow for blow was a fine test of stamina and guts. But it was no test at all of imagination. In dealing with tough customers, creativity is a better way of doing business.

Two Common Mistakes

COMBATIVE BUYERS ARE hard enough to handle without provoking them further, yet many salespeople unintentionally annoy buyers to the point of complete exasperation. What's worse, the two most common mistakes crop up most frequently at times of disagreement, the very moment when poking sticks at the customer ought to be the last item on your list of priorities.

The first mistake is belaboring. Some salespeople will repeat a single point until customers begin to feel badgered or heckled. Chances are they heard you the first time. You can also belabor a customer with logic or with constant explanations that seem to suggest that the customer is none too bright.

The second mistake is rebutting every point your customer makes, which is almost certain to lead to argument—point and counterpoint. Don't say "night" every time your customer says "day," even if you're convinced the customer is wrong.

Originally published in November–December 1988
Reprint 88605

*Author's note: I wish to acknowledge the ideas of Ann Carol Brown,
David Berlew, John Carlisle, Greg Crawford, Richard Pascale, Mike
Pedler, Neil Rackham, and my colleagues at the Forum Corporation.*

Turning Negotiation into a Corporate Capability

DANNY ERTEL

Executive Summary

EVERY COMPANY TODAY exists in a complex web of relationships formed, one at a time, through negotiation. Purchasing and outsourcing contracts are negotiated with vendors. Marketing arrangements are negotiated with distributors. Product development agreements are negotiated with joint-venture partners. Taken together, the thousands of negotiations a typical company engages in have an enormous effect on both its strategy and its bottom line.

But few companies think systematically about their negotiating activities as a whole. Instead they take a situational view, perceiving each negotiation to be a separate event with its own goals, tactics, and measures of success. Coordinating them all seems an overwhelming and impracticable job.

In reality, the author argues, it is neither. A number of companies are successfully building coordinated negotiation capabilities by applying four broad changes in practice and perspective. First, they've established a company-wide negotiation infrastructure to apply the knowledge gained from forging past agreements to improve future ones. Second, they've broadened the measures they use to evaluate negotiators' performance beyond matters of cost and price. Third, they draw a clear distinctions between the elements of an individual deal and the nature of the ongoing relationship between the parties. Fourth, they make their negotiators feel comfortable walking away from a deal when it's not in the company's best interests.

These changes aren't radical steps. But taken together, they will let companies establish closer, more creative relationships with suppliers, customers, and other partners.

E~VERY COMPANY TODAY~ exists in a complex web of relationships, and the shape of that web is formed, one thread at a time, through negotiations. Purchasing and outsourcing contracts are negotiated with suppliers. Marketing arrangements are negotiated with domestic and foreign distributors. The contents of product and service bundles are negotiated with customers. Product development pacts are negotiated with joint-venture partners. It's difficult to think of any business initiative that does not require some form of negotiation.

Although the outcome of any single negotiation may not have much effect on a business's fortunes, the thousands of negotiations a typical company undertakes have, in combination, an enormous impact on its strategy and its bottom line. In my years of consulting on negotiations, however, I have found that companies rarely think systematically about their negotiating activities as a whole. Rather, they take a situational view, seeing each negotiation as a separate event, with its own goals, its own tactics, and its own measures of success. That approach can produce good results in particular instances, but it can turn out to be counterproductive when viewed from a higher, more strategic plane. Hammering out advantageous terms on a procurement contract may, for example, torpedo an important long-term relationship with a supplier. Or coming up with a creative response to one customer's unusual needs may undermine a broad market or product strategy.

It's easy to understand why companies take a piecemeal view of negotiation. Each negotiating situation tends to be highly complicated in its own right. A negotiator has to balance a welter of contending factors relating to both the substance and the tactics of the negotiation. How much can I bend on price to gain a larger order? Should I strive to establish a long-term relationship, or should I concentrate on closing a short-term deal? Should I make the first offer, or should I wait for the other side to show its hand? Can I salvage this deal, or should I walk away now? It's so hard to make wise trade-offs in any one negotiation that trying to think about coordinating all your negotiations can seem overwhelming.

Executives have to move away from the situational view of negotiation to see that it can be managed at the corporate level.

But as partnerships, alliances, and other agreements become more important in business, the pressure to treat negotiation as an institutional capability, rather than as a series of discrete events, grows stronger. In response, a number of companies have begun to take a fresh look at the way they negotiate. They have found that building a strong negotiation capability is not a matter of creating a set of hard-and-fast rules for all negotiations—putting negotiators in bureaucratic strait-jackets won't work. Rather, it requires a different, more coordinated approach to organizing and managing negotiations. Executives have to move away from the situational view of negotiation—they have to see that negotiation can be managed at a corporate level.

In my experience, the companies that have successfully built a negotiation capability have done so through four broad changes in practice and perspective. First, they have put a companywide negotiation infrastructure in place, ensuring that negotiators' priorities remain tightly linked to the company's priorities. Second, they have broadened the measures used to evaluate negotiators' performance beyond matters of cost and price. Third, they draw a clear distinction between individual deals and ongoing relationships. And, finally, they make their negotiators feel comfortable walking away from a deal that is not in the company's overall best interest.

Creating a Negotiation Infrastructure

Negotiation is one of the few functions in the modern corporation that has resisted the trend toward standardizing processes and streamlining work. While companies have reengineered customer service, manufacturing, and even research and development, they have allowed negotiation to remain the realm of the individual. Each negotiation is viewed as a separate event, and its outcome is thought to depend on the negotiator's personal judgment, timing, and experience.

Negotiators, of course, have a vested interest in the notion that every negotiation is unique. It isolates them from interference and criticism. If the negotiation is a success, they reap all the praise. If it's a failure, they can shrug and say, "You had to be there." And when a manager, trying to be supportive, pats the negotiator on the back and says, "Put it behind you; you'll get them next time," the manager becomes an unwitting coconspirator in perpetuating the situational view.

In reality, the outcome of a negotiation does not hinge solely on the negotiator's individual skills.

In fact, the outcome of a negotiation does not hinge solely on the negotiator's individual skills. Negotiation can be coordinated and supported like any other function. Grupo Financiero Serfin, one of Mexico's largest banks, recently found that out during a time of extreme hardship. Like most other Mexican banks, Serfin faced a large number of loan defaults in the wake of the country's 1994 currency crisis. In response, Serfin's negotiating teams followed the pattern typical of loan workouts: They sat down with each debtor and traded concessions over what percentage of the loan would be repaid, when, and with what conditions. They backed up their positions with occasional threats of legal action. But despite the bank's considerable investments in hiring additional staff and providing some basic training, the negotiations did not succeed in improving the overall health of the bank's loan portfolio.

Desperate to improve the performance of the negotiators, the bank decided to take a new tack. It looked for opportunities to standardize and codify its negotiation processes, to impose some management controls, and to change the negotiators' concession-oriented culture. In short, it set about to build a corporate infrastructure for negotiations.

As a first step, Serfin developed and rolled out an improved negotiation-training curriculum that focused on putting trainees into real-world situations. But then the bank went much further. It required that negotiation considerations be incorporated into the initial financial analysis of each workout case. Collaborating closely with the responsible negotiating team, Serfin's analysts defined the bank's various interests in the case, put them in order of priority, developed an understanding of each of the debtor's interests, laid out a set of creative options for resolving the case, and assessed the debtor's and the bank's alternatives to reaching a negotiated settlement. The entire analysis of the case became a blueprint for its eventual negotiation.

To aid in the analysis, the bank also created a categorization scheme, rating each debtor according to four criteria: the debtor's ability to repay its loans over both the short and the long term, the quality of its relationship with the bank, the quality of its collateral, and the quality of the bank's best alternative to reaching a settlement. The category into which a debtor falls suggests an appropriate negotiation strategy. For example, a debtor who has a good relationship with the bank and whose ability to repay stands to improve over time, but whose collateral is weak, would warrant a highly collaborative, creative approach. A debtor whose relationship with the bank is strained but whose collateral and ability to repay are strong would require an approach that focuses on strengthening the underlying relationship. A debtor whose ability to repay is weak and who has a poor relationship with the bank would warrant a more confrontational approach, with a strong threat of foreclosure.

To help the negotiating teams carry out their strategies, the company set up a system for sharing successful practices. Negotiators in each of the bank's five workout divisions were asked to identify their 20 toughest cases. The team responsible for each case then gathered with negotiators from the other divisions, and, together with a negotiation coach, they reviewed the case in depth, analyzing what had happened to date and what they might do next. The sessions produced a set of lessons that was shared with all the bank's negotiators and was also used to refine the categorization scheme. This exercise not only helped the negotiators conduct subsequent negotiations but also reinforced the idea that negotiation is an institutional process that can be evaluated and fine-tuned systematically.

Serfin's efforts to establish a negotiation infrastructure dramatically changed the way its negotiators viewed their roles and did their jobs. Far from being a straitjacket, the infrastructure led to a burst of creativity. Guided by the bank's overall interests, Serfin's workout teams became innovative problem solvers, working in partnership with debtors. One exemplary case involved a large loan to a manufacturer that had long been a major borrower. The negotiating team worked with the debtor's managers to find a third-party investor who was willing to take an equity stake in the company. By shoring up the company's finances, the negotiators were able to help it back to health, not only saving the loan but reinvigorating the lending relationship. In the past, the negotiating team would simply have bought time by restructuring the debt, knowing that the company would soon be in default again. As a result of its innovative practices, Serfin's workout division is today considered the best in the country, a model for other institutions.

There are many other equally straightforward ways to begin building a negotiation infrastructure. One prominent professional-services firm is developing a centralized database to help its project managers negotiate scope-and-fee agreements with clients. Every time a manager negotiates with a client, he or she will now be expected to fill out a brief questionnaire that captures the approaches taken, the results achieved, and the lessons learned. The answers will be entered into the database, which other project managers can then tap into when preparing for their own negotiations. Rather than acting as lone wolves, project managers will be able to inform their own strategies and actions with the collective wisdom of their colleagues. They will also be able to use the database as a "negotiation yellow pages," identifying colleagues with useful experience and expertise. As an added benefit, the database will generate periodic reports for management highlighting the tactics and outcomes of negotiations, and these reports will enable the firm to further refine its understanding of what works and what doesn't in bargaining with clients.

The management tools don't have to be high tech. At another professional-services firm—one of the Big Five accountancies—every partner is expected to engage at least one other partner in a pricing consultation before negotiating fees on any major new engagement. The partners help each other get ready for the negotiation, and they share experiences about the success or failure of prior negotiations conducted under similar circumstances.

At one highly successful software company, the senior vice president of sales has established a set of negotiation protocols for all sales representatives. The protocols lay out steps to be taken in preparing for and conducting negotiations, and they require that the reps be debriefed after each negotiation, ensuring that the company captures important information. The protocols include establishing both sides' options in order of priority, considering multiple options in the course of the negotiation, and using a set of objective criteria to shape the discussion.

The actions these companies have taken are for the most part modest—providing more and better information to negotiators, drawing lessons from past negotiations, setting up categorization and prioritization schemes to guide negotiators in selecting their strategies, conducting regular evaluations using standard criteria. But by creating a broadly supportive infrastructure, they produce powerful results. They don't just improve the outcomes of individual negotiations; they break down the assumption that every negotiation is unique and immune to coordination and control. They form the basis for more collaboration, creativity, and efficiency—not to mention more accountability—throughout a company's negotiation activities.

Broadening the Measures of Success

The way a company measures the success of a negotiation guides the way a negotiator approaches and conducts the negotiation. Although many companies have begun to stress the importance of forging partnerships with key suppliers and customers, in most cases this goal remains a high-level aspiration that has not been translated into clear performance measures for negotiations. Most measures still center on gaining the best price or achieving the lowest cost. Dollars and cents, after all, are the easiest things to measure, and they form a concrete basis for setting budget goals and for linking negotiators' pay to their performance.

Emphasizing financial measures naturally leads negotiators to focus on cost issues. Consider what happens in most procurement departments. Each year, budget goals are established that assume certain (usually fairly aggressive) price targets will be met for goods purchased. Knowing that they'll be judged according to how well they meet or beat these targets, department managers instruct the purchasing agents to get the best possible prices from suppliers, and they evaluate each deal according to some measure of price—the discount from the list or the prevailing market price, for instance. Knowing they'll be judged on the price breaks they achieve, the purchasers view negotiation as a zero-sum game—for them to win, the other side has to lose. Even if the company espouses a win-win approach in dealing with vendors, the purchasers know that their managers will be amply satisfied if they can bring home a big discount.

Focusing on discounts has an insidious effect on purchasing agents' behavior. It leads them to ignore opportunities to be innovative in working with suppliers to create new value by, for example, reducing inventories, developing higher-quality components, or communicating electronically. That can hamstring a company's attempts to make strategic changes that require new, more collaborative relationships with suppliers, such as moving to a build-to-order manufacturing system. Furthermore, it undermines the parties' ability to deal effectively with unexpected problems. If a supplier feels that it lost out in a negotiation with a customer—that it was squeezed by the customer—then when the customer has a problem later on, the supplier is likely to respond with indifference at best and downright hostility at worst.

One large engineering and architectural-services company—I'll call it Acme Engineering—has adopted a broader way of measuring success in negotiations. It evaluates a negotiation according to seven diverse standards that focus as much on process as on outcome. (See "A New Set of Measures" at the end of this article.) To be judged successful, negotiators have to show, for example, that they established a climate of open communication with the other party, that they explicitly discussed several creative alternatives, that they used objective criteria to choose among the alternatives, and that the final deal fulfills not only the company's interests but the other parties' as well.

It might be argued that these kinds of measures are soft and difficult to quantify—but that's just the point. Because they're not cut-and-dried, they force negotiators and their managers to think more broadly and creatively about negotiations, both when strategies are initially established and as the bargaining unfolds. When negotiations become complicated or difficult, negotiators can't simply fall back to trading concessions. They have to balance a host of considerations, which leads them to explore more options and to hold wider-ranging discussions.

Of course, establishing the right measures is only half the challenge. You also have to link those measures to the incentives that will actually govern negotiators' behavior. To encourage broader, more creative negotiations, a number of companies are expanding the criteria they use to determine purchasing agents' and salespeople's bonuses and commissions. On the procurement side, they are seeking to tie incentives not to the price discounts achieved but to the total cost of ownership of the purchased good, taking into account the operating efficiencies gained through using the supplier, the reductions in defects achieved by the supplier, and even the supplier's role in developing product or service innovations. On the sales side, they are exploring ways to base a significant portion of sales reps' compensation on the longevity of their customer relationships, the innovations that have resulted from their interactions with customers, customers' own evaluations of those relationships, and the referral business that can be traced to those customers.

Motivation can come from nonfinancial rewards as well. In recent years, many companies have set up programs to capture and share knowledge. To encourage employees to participate, they frequently give out various kinds of prizes—even something as simple as a mousepad—to anyone who contributes to or draws on the knowledge banks. Such tokens of appreciation signal the importance management places on the effort and, in time, help build a culture in which sharing knowledge is the norm. Companies may want to think about giving similar awards to those whose day-to-day negotiations with customers, suppliers, and others generate new ideas or otherwise create unusual value. Anything that can jar people out of the concession-bargaining mind-set should be viewed as useful.

Distinguishing Between the Deal and the Relationship

Broader performance measures can get negotiators to look beyond the immediate deal to the larger relationship. But if they don't draw a clear distinction between the components of the deal and the components of the relationship, they can still run into trouble. It's common for negotiators to confuse the deal and the relationship. They fear that if they push too hard to get the best deal possible today, they may jeopardize their company's ability to do business with the other party in the future. Or they fear that if they pay too much attention to the relationship, they'll end up giving away too much and make a lousy deal. Though natural, such confusion is dangerous. It leaves the negotiator open to manipulation by the other side.

Look at what routinely happens to accounting firms. A big client will tell its accountant that the firm has to cut its fees or else the work will be put out to bid. In the face of such a threat, the accountant, after defending the quality of the firm's services and pointing out the cost of switching auditors, will offer up at least a small price break for the sake of the relationship. The discount may be enough to enable the firm to hang onto the account in the short run, but that's rarely the end of the story. In another year or two, the client will be demanding another price cut in exchange for its continued business. And, having established a precedent, the accountant will once again give in.

Without realizing it, many companies have systematically taught their customers the art of blackmail.

Over the years, I have asked hundreds of executives to reflect on their business relationships and to ask themselves which kinds of customers they make more concessions to, do more costly favors for, and generally give away more value to. Is it their good customers or their difficult customers? The vast majority respond, with some chagrin, "The difficult ones, of course. I'm hoping to improve the relationship." But that hope is almost always in vain: once customers find that they can get discounts and favors by holding a relationship hostage, why should they change? Without realizing it, many companies have systematically taught their customers the art of blackmail.

The source of the problem lies in the notion that the relationship and the deal function like a seesaw: to improve one, you have to be willing to sacrifice the other. The reality is that while relationships and deals are indeed linked, they are more likely to move up or down in tandem. A strong relationship creates trust, which allows the parties to share information more freely, which in turn leads to more creative and valuable agreements and to a greater willingness to continue working together. But when a deal is struck that is not very attractive to one or both parties, chances are that they will invest less time and effort in working together, they will become more wary in communicating with each other, and their relationship will grow strained or unravel; as a result, they will be less able to take chances that would create more value. (See the exhibit "The Deal-Relationship Cycle.")

To build strong working relationships and negotiate good deals, companies need to break the pattern of trading off one for the other and begin to pay attention to each separately. They need to get their negotiators to see that a problem with a relationship cannot be resolved through concessions and that a problem with a deal should not be considered a test of the relationship. By drawing a clear line between the immediate deal and the longer-term relationship, two companies can start to create a virtuous cycle. Building a strong relationship will help them through the rough spots in a particular deal, and the value created by closing the deal will further enhance and broaden their relationship.[1]

When Eastman Kodak transferred its data center operations to IBM, the two companies struggled to balance the deal and the relationship. A lot of money was at stake, and both sides wanted the terms of the deal to be in their best interest. Kodak wanted to reduce its costs; IBM wanted to increase its revenues. But the companies also knew that the ultimate success of the outsourcing arrangement would hinge on the health and openness of their long-term relationship.

Rather than treat the deal and the relationship as intertwined, the companies separated the two explicitly. Key managers from each side sat down and first laid out what particular benefits they hoped to achieve through the terms of the immediate agreement. They then articulated as precisely as possible what would constitute a successful relationship over the long haul. On the basis of those discussions, they developed two discrete lists of issues, one relating to the terms of the deal and one relating to the nature of the relationship. (See the exhibit "Kodak and IBM: A Good Deal and a Strong Relationship.") They agreed that any problem arising from the issues on one list could not be resolved by exacting concessions on issues from the other list. Trouble with a lack of trust or poor communication—relationship issues—could not, for example, be solved through changes in pricing, software-licensing terms, or other deal-related issues. This clear distinction between the deal and the relationship guided Kodak and IBM through the initial negotiation and has continued to define their interactions. It's no coincidence that their relationship has come to be viewed as a model of effective partnering in business.

Negotiation strategies that make trade-offs between the value you can obtain in a deal and the quality of your relationship with the other party are flawed from the start. Managers who accept explanations like "To maintain the relationship, I gave in on price" from their negotiators are condoning both poor deals and weak relationships.

Learning to Walk Away from a Deal

Negotiators, like salespeople, believe that their success hinges on their ability to close deals. If a negotiation falls apart, they see it as a failure—for themselves and for their

---

The Deal-Relationship Cycle

The Usual Way

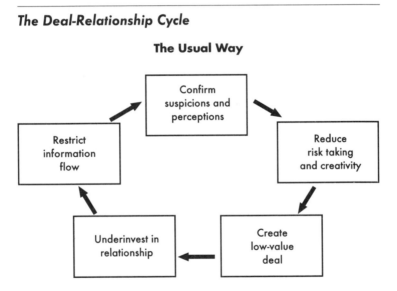

Many negotiators make the mistake of confusing the deal with the broader relationship. To improve a strained relationship, for example, they may offer a concession on price. Or to gain a price concession, they may threaten to terminate the relationship. But such an approach almost always backfires. It creates an adversarial dynamic: Negotiators withhold information to protect their bargaining positions. That leads to greater suspicion and less creativity, which in turn undermines both the immediate deal and the long-term relationship.

companies. Their reasoning is easy to understand. By the time most negotiators sit down at the bargaining table, their organizations have already invested a lot of time and money in preparation. They've analyzed their own needs, evaluated potential suppliers or partners, created and reviewed a shortlist, selected a finalist, and charted out a bargaining strategy. As the negotiators see it, failing to conclude the deal would waste all that effort, not to mention disrupt what has likely become a well-established schedule. Once a negotiation has begun, going back to the drawing board no longer seems a viable option.

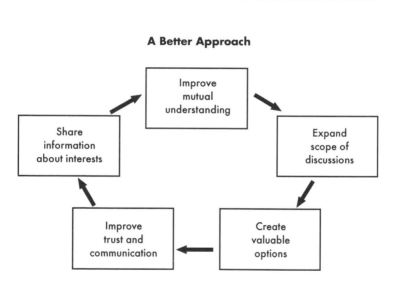

A Better Approach

A better approach is to separate the deal from the relationship. When negotiators don't feel as though they need to trade the quality of the relationship for the terms of each individual deal, they exchange information more freely and become more creative and collaborative in their discussions. That leads both to more valuable deals and to stronger, more trusting relationships.

While understandable, that kind of thinking often puts a company's negotiators in a box. They become stuck in a cycle of concessions, allowing the other side to dictate the details of the deal. At one respected South American metropolitan newspaper, for example, the advertising sales force has developed a deeply ingrained never-lose-a-client culture. The salespeople routinely offer steep discounts from their standard ad rates just to keep advertisers from walking away. Their *average* discount rate, across a $300 million advertising space, is 45%. Asked to justify the discounts, they point to the small marginal cost of producing an extra page of print.

Kodak and IBM: A Good Deal and a Strong Relationship

When Eastman Kodak and IBM negotiated an outsourcing agreement for the operation of Kodak's data centers, they carefully distinguished between the terms of the deal and the nature of the long-term relationship they hoped to engender. They developed two lists of issues—one relating to the deal, the other to the relationship—and agreed to keep the two sets of issues separate at all times. Following are illustrative excerpts from the two lists.

Deal Issues	Relationship Issues
Retirement and replacement of hardware	Reliability
Use of third-party software	Giving each other the benefit of the doubt
Service levels	Absence of coercion
Ease of communication	Understanding each other's objectives
Record storage, maintenance, and security	Timeliness of consultations
Pricing	Mutual respect
Terms of employee transfers	
Termination and return of data center operations to Kodak or transfer to another party	

As long as the ad revenue exceeds the marginal cost, they argue, the paper is coming out ahead. What they don't consider, though, is how their behavior has led advertisers to expect ever greater discounts. The advertisers, knowing the paper will do anything to keep them, have all the leverage. Each heavily discounted ad may indeed be marginally profitable, but in combination they reduce the paper's overall revenue and profits dramatically.

To get out of this box, managers need to make sure negotiators understand that they always have alternatives to closing a deal. Nearly 20 years ago, Roger Fisher and William Ury introduced into the negotiation lexicon the term "BATNA," an acronym for "Best Alternative to Negotiated Agreement." They showed that negotiation results can be greatly improved by identifying the best alternative to completing the deal and then carefully evaluating the negotiated agreement against that alternative. If the negotiated agreement is better, close the deal. If the alternative is better, walk away.[2]

The BATNA approach changes the ground rules of negotiation. Negotiators no longer see their role as producing agreements but rather as making good choices. And if they don't reach an agreement, they don't see that as a failure. If they reject a deal because it falls short of their company's BATNA, they have succeeded, not failed.

Negotiators should always think through their alternatives before they even start to negotiate. By identifying a BATNA at the outset, they establish an objective hurdle that any negotiated agreement has to clear. They don't have to rely on subjective judgments that an offer seems too low or unreasonable. As the negotiation proceeds, they should constantly think about ways to improve their BATNA—by doing further research, by considering alternative investments, or by identifying other potential allies. And they should never accept an agreement that is not at least as good as their BATNA.

Sometimes, there is no obvious alternative to a deal. In such cases, the company needs to think about creating a BATNA for itself; it shouldn't just sit back and negotiate from a position of weakness. Consider the example of Colbún SA, the third largest producer of electric power in Chile. Much smaller than its two biggest competitors, both of which are vertically integrated, Colbún has often found itself at a substantial disadvantage in terms of scale and negotiating leverage. It had to bargain for transmission capacity, for example, with the transmission arm of the largest power company. If it had gone into those negotiations without an alternative, it would have been at the mercy of the other side, and it would have ended up paying dearly for the capacity. But Colbún had an express corporate policy requiring the establishment of a BATNA in any negotiation. Because there were no other existing options for purchasing transmission capacity, Colbún had to create one—developing its own transmission line.

Executives can't just proclaim that it's okay to walk away from a deal; they need to back their rhetoric with action.

While negotiations with the dominant producer continued, Colbún developed conceptual plans for its own transmission line, conducted feasibility studies, and even put construction contracts out to bid. As development of Colbún's BATNA progressed, the other side steadily reduced its price quote—though Colbún ultimately decided it would be best served by going ahead and building its own line.

Colbún has used a similar BATNA-based strategy in many other important deals, including negotiating the purchase of turbines for a new gas-fired power plant and the transportation of natural gas to the plant. As it did in the transmission-line decision, it has in a number of instances broken off negotiations and pursued its BATNA instead.

Adopting the BATNA approach involves overturning long-held assumptions. Senior executives can't just proclaim that it's now okay to walk away from a deal; they have to make sure that the message is reinforced all the way down the chain of command. Consider what happened to one company that decided to pursue a new market strategy. From now on, the company's senior executives announced, the company would concentrate on selling only to customers to whom it could deliver high-value-added services at premium prices. Before closing a sale, salespeople should consider whether the prospective customer would meet the new criterion; if not, they should reject the deal and devote the company's resources elsewhere. In the field, however, managers continued to encourage their negotiators to discount heavily if necessary to win or maintain large accounts. The negotiators were still hearing the message "Don't let any big deal get away," and they did not change their behavior at the bargaining table. The new strategy never got off the ground.

Executives need to back up their rhetoric with actions that have an impact in the field. They need to seek out examples in which the company's negotiators decided the organization would be better served by walking away from the deal to pursue their BATNA—and then they have to praise those negotiators and use their approaches as models. If negotiators are not made aware that their colleagues are turning away some deals to pursue other opportunities, they will not believe they truly have that alternative. Companies should also consider making a BATNA evaluation an explicit step in the negotiation process, requiring, for example, that negotiators discuss with their managers how each proposed deal stacks up against a clearly defined BATNA. If negotiators are not required to assess their deals with reference to their BATNA, they may not believe the choice between the two is real.

Not only do executives have to send the right messages internally, they need to be aware of how their external communications may affect negotiators. In an interview published in a widely read magazine, the CEO of a large computer company once stated that back when he was a sales representative, he never lost a customer. He was trying to counter criticism that the company had gotten so big that it had lost sight of the customer. But imagine how the statement was interpreted by the company's sales force. The CEO was in effect telling the sales reps that they could never say no—and signaling customers that they held all the leverage. The negotiators' BATNAs were instantly rendered inconsequential with one simple public statement.

Companies routinely review public statements for their effect on stock valuation or regulatory compliance. And while I know of no company that has put in place a formal mechanism to review public statements for their effect on negotiations, it may not be such a bad idea. At the very least, those with responsibility for negotiations should alert senior executives and public relations departments to the fact that even the best-intentioned statements can subtly undermine negotiating strategies.

Little Steps to Big Changes

Shifting from a situational to an institutional view of negotiation may represent a radical change for many companies. It certainly represents a radical change for many negotiators. But it doesn't require radical actions. It requires carefully planned, often subtle, changes in practice, in emphasis, and in communication. In fact, trying to ram the new way of working down negotiators' throats, without adequate explanation or support, will just backfire, leaving negotiators confused and alienated. If, for example, management suddenly announces that all negotiators must follow a set of rigid procedures or fill out a set of forms after every meeting, negotiators will simply complain that the bureaucracy is keeping them from doing real work. They may fulfill the new requirements in a perfunctory manner, but they won't change their perspective or their behavior.

The key to success is putting the negotiation infrastructure in place that makes the lives of negotiators easier and makes their jobs more rewarding. Supplying negotiators with practical information makes it simpler for them to prepare for negotiations while also exposing them to a larger set of proven strategies so they can do more than merely trade concessions. Showing them how the BATNA approach can be used in real-world situations gives them a new source of leverage in their negotiations. Broadening the measures used to judge their performance allows them greater—not less—freedom in crafting agreements. Establishing categorization and prioritization schemes can increase their productivity and free them to think more creatively. (See the exhibit "Making Negotiation an Institutional Capability.")

Some negotiators will not be able to adapt to the new, more standardized and coordinated approaches—they'll chafe under even the lightest managerial yoke. Most, though, will thrive in the new environment. They will come to find that they have actually gained more power, more prestige, and—not least—more satisfaction. And

Making Negotiation an Institutional Capability

To move from a situational view of negotiation to one that recognizes negotiation as an institutional process does not require radical organizational change. It does require putting in place new tools and procedures that will enable executives to better manage and support negotiators.

Steps in the Negotiation Process	Situational View	Institutional View	Examples of Tools and Procedures
Determining objectives	Goals are set on a case-by-case basis; negotiators seek to maximize personal compensation.	Objectives for each negotiation are tied to larger corporate goals; separate goals are established for the deal and the relationship.	· Deal and relationship scorecards · Negotiation instructions template
Preparing for the negotiation	Preparations proceed in an ad hoc manner; often there's no time for any preparation.	Preparations are well structured; negotiators draw on prior corporate experience.	· Database of past negotiations · Worksheet for understanding counterpart's choice · Manager's checklist for BATNA review

Conducting the negotiation	Negotiators act as lone wolves with little supervision; success or failure is seen to depend on personal ability.	Managers play an active coaching role; colleagues share a negotiation approach and vocabulary.	· Negotiation playbook that links strategies to categories of negotiations · Training programs for negotiators and their managers · "Yellow Pages" that enable efficient consultation with experienced colleagues
Reviewing the negotiation	Reviews are done sporadically; focus is on cost reductions and percentage of deals closed.	Reviews are performed systematically to capture information so it can be applied to future negotiations; focus is not only on the results of each negotiation but on the way it was conducted; reviews extract lessons rather than apportion blame or praise.	· Structured review questions that focus not only on outcomes but also on process · Debriefing forms that feed into best-practices database · Training in constructive debriefing

their companies will reap the benefits of closer, more creative relationships with suppliers, customers, and other partners.

A New Set of Measures

ONE LARGE ENGINEERING and architectural-services company has gotten more out of its negotiations by broadening the way it defines success. Rather than aiming simply to book more business at higher hourly rates, the company uses seven criteria in reviewing negotiations:

Relationship: Does the negotiation process help build the kind of relationship that will enable us and our clients to work effectively together over the project's life cycle?

Communication: Do our negotiations help create an environment in which both parties can engage in constructive conversations aimed at solving problems?

Interests: Have we crafted a deal that satisfies our interests well at the same time that it satisfies our client's interests to at least an acceptable level and the interests of any relevant third parties (government regulators, environmental groups, and so on) to at least a tolerable level?

Options: As part of the negotiation process, have we searched for innovative, elegant, and efficient solutions that might offer joint gains?

Legitimacy: After brainstorming a variety of options, have we used objective criteria to evaluate and choose an option that could be justified by both sides?

BATNA: Have we measured the proposed deal against our Best Alternative to Negotiated Agreement, and are we confident that it satisfies our interests better than our BATNA does?

Commitment: Have we generated a set of well-planned, realistic, and workable commitments that both sides understand and are prepared to implement?

Taken together, these criteria serve not only as standards for evaluating the success of any negotiation but also as a checklist that the company's deal makers can use in preparing for negotiations.

Notes

1. For further discussion on separating the deal from the relationship, see Roger Fisher and Scott Brown, *Getting Together: Building a Relationship That Gets to Yes* (Boston: Houghton Mifflin, 1988).

2. The concept of BATNA was introduced by Roger Fisher and William L. Ury in *Getting to Yes: Negotiating Agreement Without Giving In* (Houghton Mifflin, 1981). Its successful application has been extensively documented by the negotiation scholar Howard Raiffa, among others. See, for example, Raiffa's classic *The Art and Science of Negotiation* (Cambridge, Mass.: Belknap Press, 1982).

Originally published in May–June 1999
Reprint 99304

When Consultants and Clients Clash

IDALENE F. KESNER AND
SALLY FOWLER

Executive Summary

THIS FICTITIOUS CASE STUDY explores the issues that surround the relationships between consultants and their clients, as well as the dynamics of a newly merged organization.

Susan Barlow, a senior consultant with the Statler Group, dreaded her upcoming status meeting. She had thought it a lucky break when she got assigned to the Kellogg-Champion project. Royce Kellogg, the CEO of the newly merged firm, had engaged the Statler Group for what seemed a simple project: to reconcile the policies and practices of the two former firms now that they had become one. But once on the job, Barlow realized that the issues were much more complex than they had seemed. The new firm needed help badly—but not the kind of help that the client had led Barlow to believe it needed. What would she and Jim Roussos, her partner on the assignment, tell Kellogg at the meeting?

Kellogg, for his part was not looking forward to the status meeting, either. From his point of view, the consultants had caused more problems than they had solved. What's more, he wasn't even dealing with the consultants he had hired. Where was George Gray, the senior partner he had met with originally? Maybe Barlow and Roussos were just too young and inexperienced. Kellogg felt he was getting a raw deal. How would he approach them in the morning? Should he fire them or make an attempt at damage control?

Two experts advise the consultants and two advise the client on how to handle the status meeting.

The Consultant's Side of the Story

"How did I ever get myself into this situation?" Susan Barlow said, sighing in frustration. Less than 12 hours remained until an 8 A.M. status meeting with the most misguided and cantankerous client she'd ever worked for, and Barlow was sitting in her office, drumming her fingers on her well-organized desk. Neat piles of policy documents and transcribed interviews obscured the project management flowchart she had drawn for the Kellogg-Champion project, and she pulled it free to inspect it for what seemed like the hundredth time.

Where was Jim with the take-out menus? Once they had eaten, they could get down to business. Between the two of them, they should be able to figure out a defensible course of action fairly quickly. After all, the Kellogg-Champion Securities engagement had seemed like such a straightforward job—at first.

Indeed, when the Kellogg-Champion opportunity had dropped into her lap, Barlow, a senior consultant with the Statler Group, thought it a lucky break. She was happy when she got the call from her director of human resources. The conversation had been brief and to the point: Kellogg & Meyer had merged with Champion Securities. The new CEO of Kellogg-Champion, Royce Kellogg, had engaged the Statler Group for a fairly simple job: to reconcile the policies and practices of the two former firms now that they had become Kellogg-Champion. Another senior consultant assigned to the case had suddenly resigned for personal reasons, and Barlow's background in the securities industry made her the ideal replacement. The Statler Group and Kellogg had already agreed on fees and a schedule, but the project had not yet begun. Could Barlow fill in?

Barlow had been particularly enthusiastic because the consulting firm had recently decided to target the securities industry as a new source of growth. And although she had never dealt with a merger before, six years of successful consulting experience told her that the task would consist mostly of comparing two sets of policies in detail and then touching base with the relevant managers. She had thought she would be able to crack the case quickly if she pushed through the grunt work fast enough—and the project's profitability depended on speed. Jim Roussos, a junior consultant with two years' tenure at Statler, would be working with her, she had learned in that initial phone conversation. Roussos had been assigned to the project from the start. Thinking back now, Barlow sighed again. She wished she could say that Roussos or any other single factor was responsible for the mess they were in, but she couldn't. From day one, Roussos had shown himself to be a hard worker.

Finding the flowchart useless, Barlow tossed it aside. Every deadline had slipped. How could such a simple project go awry? What had she done wrong? And where were those dratted menus? She was starving.

SEEMED LIKE A GOOD IDEA AT THE TIME

Barlow thought back to the kickoff meeting that had taken place almost immediately after she accepted the assignment—a mere two weeks earlier. Although Royce Kellogg had struck Barlow as overconfident and patronizing in that first meeting, she remembered shrugging off his behavior as typical of an entrepreneur-turned-CEO. "Maybe I should have taken some of his grandstanding more seriously," she thought with a twinge of regret. "Maybe he really meant some of the stuff that I wrote off as corporate platitudes."

She tried to remember Kellogg's exact words—something like, "Although my firm acquired Champion Securities and I am its chairman and CEO, the integration of our two firms is a merger of equals. Each of the firms contributes important strengths to the combination, and all our employees know that." Barlow remembered smiling in encouragement at the banalities. After all, he was the client.

Barlow also recalled Kellogg's explanation of why the postmerger integration had gone so smoothly. It all had sounded like a well-worn lecture to her: "The secret is careful planning before the two come together, and good communication from start to finish." Then he added, "Because the big integration-related issues have been resolved, the only thing that remains to be done is finalizing common operating policies and procedures in ways that are good business and fair to all involved." Clearly, Kellogg had believed that the job of merging policies and procedures would be simple. And he had also made it clear that because both sets of policies were the same in many respects, he didn't see the need to create any new policies.

"I have already notified key employees that you will be calling, and I've asked them to give you their full cooperation," he had added. "Be sure to touch base with folks from both sides so that nobody feels left out."

When Barlow had received the list of people to contact, she began to wonder whether everything really was as simple as it appeared. Were all these people truly in agreement? She read the newspapers—since when had a merger ever gone so smoothly? But Barlow also knew that Kellogg had built his original firm from nothing into a huge success, and he seemed like the kind of forceful leader who could plow through anything and make it work. So voicing none of her doubts, Barlow had agreed to the schedule with outward enthusiasm: a status meeting to discuss any problems in two weeks and a final report in a month.

TWENTY-TWENTY HINDSIGHT

Barlow now wished that she and Roussos had accomplished more during the first week. She had spent the first two days after the kickoff meeting extricating herself from another project while Roussos collected and organized the myriad documents that formed the policies and procedures of Kellogg & Meyer and its rival, Champion Securities. In what remained of the week, they had identified policies that were the same and developed a detailed list of differences. The list of differences outweighed the list of similarities by a fairly large margin.

Barlow winced when she remembered how surprised she and Roussos had been by the number of discrepancies. Why hadn't warning bells gone off then?

And why hadn't she and Roussos been more concerned about how hard it was to schedule interviews with the major players? Two of those employees had called Kellogg's office to find out if it was okay to talk to "these outsiders." When Roussos had joked, "Kellogg's brilliant communication about the merger may have stopped at the outer door of headquarters' inner sanctum," Barlow had laughed grimly and vowed to work harder. She remembered that she had decided to focus first on the sensitive area of compensation policy: better to identify the biggest problems and deal with them as soon as possible.

FROM BAD TO WORSE

The first conversation—the one that set the unhappy tone for the others—had been with Carol Ludwig, the polite but brisk director of human resources from Kellogg & Meyer. When Barlow had asked Ludwig her opinion about the merged firm's compensation policy, Ludwig answered coolly that she could save everybody a lot of time by simply referring them to Kellogg & Meyer's policy manual. "We revised our compensation system just before the merger to make it truly state-of-the-art," she had explained. "Champion's outmoded compensation system no longer meets the organization's needs."

According to Ludwig, Champion's brokers were "thrilled to pieces" at the prospect of switching to Kellogg & Meyer's compensation system. But Barlow and Roussos hadn't had a chance to question her more closely about that assertion. Ludwig's secretary had interrupted them after only 20 minutes to announce the director's next appointment. And as Ludwig hurried the consultants out of her office, Barlow got the feeling that her distracted promise to answer any other questions at a more convenient time was just a way to get rid of them.

Next Barlow and Roussos had interviewed Tom Flynn. The former director of human resources for Champion Securities, Flynn hadn't had the faintest idea why the consultants wanted to talk to him. He said that Kellogg had not told him about the consultants, adding, "But that's not unusual, since I've been out of the communication loop ever since the merger. Perhaps you could let me in on Kellogg's plans?"

Barlow remembered her embarrassment when she had told Flynn that the merged firm planned to adopt Kellogg & Meyer's compensation system. His response had been angry—and loud: "You got that from Carol Ludwig, didn't you? She knows we agreed to use Champion Securities' compensation policy.

"Am I a coward or a politician?" Susan Barlow wondered ruefully in retrospect. "Maybe both."

Champion's brokers are the best in the business, and there's no way they would stand for any changes in compensation. Before the merger, Royce Kellogg promised not to change anything. Carol and I have been over this a hundred times, and the only thing we agreed to use from Kellogg & Meyer was the computer program that keeps track of compensation. Wait till Champion's brokers hear about this. We'll have mass resignations on our hands!"

Remembering that scene, Barlow realized uncomfortably that she had probably missed a chance to get inside the reality of the merger. "All I did was try to calm him down," she thought, sighing. "I just tried to pass it off as my misunderstanding. I knew very well that Ludwig clearly saw herself in the driver's seat. Why didn't I consider the implications for Flynn and for everyone else from Champion?"

Interviewing the former marketing directors of the two firms had proved equally awkward. John Tucker, senior vice president in charge of marketing for Kellogg & Meyer, had sketched out an organization chart that showed Greg Masters, executive vice president of marketing for Champion, reporting to him. The chart that Masters drew for Barlow and Roussos revealed a different understanding: Masters clearly believed that he and Tucker were on the *same* level and that *both* marketing directors reported directly to Kellogg. After the ruckus with Flynn, Barlow had decided not to mention the contradiction to either marketing man. "Am I a coward or a politician?" she wondered ruefully in retrospect. "Maybe both."

Barlow then thought back to the consultants' visits to two branch managers—one from each of the former firms. She and Roussos had hoped to find greater agreement at the operational level. "How could I have been so naïve?" she thought.

The two consultants had split the interviews between them because the branches were in different cities and time was of the essence. Barlow had interviewed Russell Sanders, the manager of one of Champion's most profitable offices. After Sanders had ushered her into his office, he closed the door, lowered his voice, and begged her to keep the conversation in the strictest confidence. "I'm sure they've told you that all the merger issues have been settled and we're all one big, happy family, but don't you believe it," he had said. "Everyone operates under their old policies, and virtually no communication exists between the management personnel of the two predecessor firms. Kellogg pats himself on the back for having done such a great job of bringing the firms together, and nobody has the intestinal fortitude to tell him that the merger has been a colossal failure."

Roussos, meanwhile, had spoken with Brian Matsuo, an office manager from Kellogg & Meyer. Matsuo had told Roussos that he was much too busy to bother with office politics and that the merger was going very well, as far as he could tell. His office followed the policies and procedures that had been in effect before the merger, and he saw no need to change anything. When Roussos had probed about specific operating policies, Matsuo referred him to the Kellogg & Meyer policy manual. "Matsuo had no intention of saying anything that deviated in the slightest from the party line," Roussos had told Barlow later that day, over the phone. Barlow had wondered privately whether she could have gotten more out of Matsuo than Roussos did. Maybe she shouldn't have sent the young consultant out alone on such a tough interview.

WHAT TO DO?

A knock at the door brought Barlow back to her most pressing need: dinner. Roussos came into the office waving three dog-eared menus. "Sorry it took so long to get back to you," he apologized with a sheepish grin. "I was trying to reconcile the various menus of each type—Chinese, Italian, ribs—to come up with an optimal list of offerings for our team."

Barlow laughed. "Let's get some *moo shu* and figure out what we're going to say to dear Mr. Kellogg in the morning."

The Client's Side Of The Story

Royce Kellogg, CEO of Kellogg-Champion Securities, stared out the window of his twelfth-floor office. It was getting late, and there wasn't much activity on the streets of downtown Dallas. Slowly, he swiveled his chair around to face the glass walls of the bull pen. Desks and equipment filled the large, open area, and the computer screens glowed eerily. It was strange to see the room so empty.

Kellogg thought about the 8 A.M. appointment the next day with the consultants from the Statler Group, and he grimaced. "I hired those people for a simple, straightforward assignment: to help blend policies and programs during the final stages of merging this firm with Champion Securities," he thought. "But those blasted consultants have caused more problems than they've solved."

As Kellogg reflected on what his organization had been through, he pounded his fist on the broad arm of his chair. "The people in this firm and I have worked too damn hard to see a couple of inexperienced consultants throw a hand grenade in the middle of everything," he thought. "If Mort were here, he'd have them for breakfast."

UNLIKELY BEDFELLOWS

Kellogg thought back to the day 34 years earlier when he and his friend and partner, Mort Meyer, had opened the doors to the brokerage house of Kellogg & Meyer. Although both men were expert in securities, Kellogg had made most of the business decisions, while Meyer had excelled at building an organization staffed with long-term, dedicated professionals. Together they had survived some lean times and a couple of nasty recessions, and the firm had earned the respect of the brokerage community from the start.

After years of steady growth, Kellogg & Meyer's business and reputation had soared in the 1980s. "When the other firms hit the skids in 1987, we knew how to handle it," Kellogg recalled proudly. Thanks largely to Kellogg's canny reading of the market, the firm's client newsletter had recommended investing 80% in cash and 20% in securities only three weeks before the thud—and many clients had gotten out of the market in the nick of time. After the crash, Kellogg & Meyer had advised its clients to load up on newly undervalued stocks—with very profitable results. Those two tips alone did more for the firm's reputation than its previous quarter century of solid performance. Kellogg & Meyer saw its accounts balloon in the five years following the crash, as it attracted larger and wealthier clients. Under Meyer's guidance, the firm managed its growth brilliantly, and its sprawling network of local branches grew even larger.

The success soon tasted bittersweet, however. Kellogg still felt keenly the loss of Meyer to a sudden heart attack three years before. "I wish Mort were here now," Kellogg thought in frustration. "He was always better at dealing with this people stuff. He was so good at keeping the firm together, making sure that folks stayed happy. I wish that Stan Carpenter had anything close to Mort's people touch."

In fact, Meyer's death had prompted the merger of Kellogg & Meyer and Champion. When Meyer's family sold its interest in the firm, Kellogg had become the largest shareholder. Soon after Meyer's death, Stan Carpenter, CEO of Champion Securities, had invited Kellogg to join him in his box at a Cowboys game, and at halftime, Carpenter had asked Kellogg the question: "What do you say we stop beating up on each other and join forces? Why don't we stop dividing up this pie and make it bigger instead?" Kellogg remembered his fleeting hesitation: he had always run his own show with a man who'd been like a brother to him. What would Kellogg & Meyer be like with Carpenter and Champion attached to it?

But Kellogg had decided to take Carpenter seriously. After all, the two firms were about equal in market share, and although Kellogg didn't like to admit it, he had known for a while that Champion was poised for faster growth than his firm was: Champion's brokers concentrated mostly on young, upwardly mobile professionals while Kellogg & Meyer's business depended on older investors. By the end of the football game, the two men had identified enough opportunities for synergy to convince Kellogg that a merger made good sense. "You may be onto something here, Stan," Kellogg remembered saying. "Costs should come down, revenues should go up, and we'd leave everyone else in the dust." Kellogg and Carpenter had met several times in the three weeks following the game.

One week later, each CEO had promised the other that he would speak to his board. Kellogg & Meyer's board had supported its CEO wholeheartedly, as they did on most issues he brought to them. Kellogg had been somewhat surprised by the challenges Carpenter's board raised—after all, was Carpenter CEO of Champion or not?—but ultimately their questions had been answered and they had approved the merger. "I guess it made sense that they'd balk at the Kellogg name coming first and at my being CEO while Stan is president," he recalled saying to his wife. "They're worried that we'll have enough board members and won't need them anymore. They have nothing to worry about—I want everyone's expertise."

IT'S NOT ROCKET SCIENCE

"I wonder if maybe we didn't hurry things a bit too much after we decided to merge," Kellogg reflected as he sank deeper into his chair. "I hope that people have had a chance to adjust." During the previous three years, several direct competitors of Kellogg & Meyer had acquired other firms, and those newly combined organizations seemed to be thriving. In the case of Kellogg & Meyer and Champion, both firms operated in the same segment of the same industry, acting as full-service agents providing a broad range of financial instruments. Even the sizes and locations of their branch offices overlapped a great deal.

Kellogg knew that it was important to speed the blending of the two cultures. He had developed a statement that he used at all public occasions: "Everyone who is in the boat has to be pulling oars in the same direction. Our two firms had unique cultures before the merger, but we all are ready to place our individual differences aside. From this point on, our firm will operate as a whole unit, not as two separate entities." When questioned by an industry analyst about the magnitude of the differences between the firms and the time it would take to integrate them, Kellogg had responded, "Look, if Stan Carpenter and I can go from rivals to partners, then surely our people can find a way to work out their differences. This isn't rocket science. We're all in the same business, and only the big guys are going to survive."

He returned to the present with a start, shaking his head. "I don't understand why this deal with these consultants is such a hassle," he thought, as he stared into the bull pen. "The differences between Kellogg & Meyer and Champion are purely internal. They are completely within our direct control: evaluation, control and compensation, office policies and procedures, hierarchical levels, reporting structures, and executive titles. This is annoying, time-consuming stuff—but it's not *difficult*. Not like figuring out derivatives!"

BRING ON THE CONSULTANTS

It was at the recommendation of business associates, Kellogg remembered, that he had decided to talk to the Statler Group. In the preliminary meeting, he had met Statler partner George Gray, senior consultant Amanda Roth, and junior consultant Jim Roussos. Accepting their proposal with little delay and only a few minor modifications, Kellogg had scheduled a kickoff meeting several weeks later.

He also remembered the flash of irritation he felt when he realized that he wouldn't get the Statler consultants he had originally met. "What was that all about, anyway?" he muttered. "Bait and switch? Bring in the partner to sell the business, then fob the client off on some kids cutting their teeth in the business world? I should have raised a fuss in the kickoff meeting." He sighed. His kids were older than Barlow and Roussos.

"If I wasn't being clear, why didn't they say so? Maybe the partner in charge didn't brief them."

Because the change in consultants had disconcerted him, he had been particularly careful to make a few critical points as powerfully as he could in that meeting. He also had given Barlow and Roussos parts of his integration speech. "I can't imagine that I didn't make myself perfectly clear," he now fumed to the empty bull pen. "I said quite clearly what these consultants could and could not do. I clearly said, 'No new policies. Simply integrate existing policies and programs. Expect full cooperation from any and all employees.' And if that wasn't clear, why didn't they say something? A couple of minor questions, your basic chitchat about the weather—that was all I got. Maybe the partner in charge never even briefed them."

STIRRING UP TROUBLE

"I should have taken the early signs of trouble more seriously," Kellogg thought, chastising himself. As soon as the consultants began conducting their interviews, he had fielded a couple of calls from employees asking what the consultants were doing and whether it was okay to talk to them. "I thought my people just wanted to know if I supported the project," he mused. "I should have taken it as a sign that something else was going on."

And things had gone rapidly downhill, Kellogg recalled now. First, Carpenter had called, wanting Kellogg to know that his people were very upset. "Royce, what gives?" Carpenter had asked. "I had to calm Tom Flynn down for an hour after the consultants blew through. Then I had to smooth Greg Masters's ruffled feathers—he wanted to know why he hadn't been consulted about mythical changes in the organization chart. And then one of my best branch managers told me that those two planned to downsize the Champion side by 50%! I had a mutiny on my hands. I can't afford to lose these guys. We've got to stop this before it becomes a runaway train."

Kellogg had received equally distressing calls from other parts of the new firm. Office manager Brian Matsuo had been particularly annoyed. "I don't know why these people are here," he had sputtered. "They act as if I'm hiding something when all I'm trying to do is minimize the normal stresses that come with any merger and go about my work."

DAMAGE CONTROL

"Damn it, I'm not getting what I paid for," Kellogg thought angrily. "Where is that Statler partner while his two junior consultants stir up trouble? Do Barlow and Roussos have the experience to operate on their own? Obviously not, if they can't handle a simple interview."

He swiveled to face his desk. "Should I keep these people on or call a halt to this farce before things get worse?" he asked himself. "If I do continue with them, how can I make my point any clearer? What can I do about the damage that has already been done?" Finally, he said aloud, "Maybe firing those clowns would signal once and for all that the rumors are false."

Then he settled down and wondered what Mort would have done.

Is the business relationship between the Statler Group and Kellogg-Champion Securities a lost cause? How should the

consultants—and the client—handle the status meeting?

Two commentators advise the consultants, and two advise the client, on whether the situation can be salvaged.

JOHN RAU *is CEO of Chicago Title & Trust Company. He is the former dean of Indiana University's School of Business in Bloomington and the former CEO of LaSalle National Bank and its predecessor, Exchange National Bank. As head of LaSalle and Exchange from 1983 to 1991, Rau presided over two of the largest full bank mergers in the state of Illinois.*

One could start with the platitude that a consultant's responsibility is to do whatever is best for the client. But here is a situation in which the client has outlined an assignment that can be executed only in a fantasy world. Royce Kellogg, the CEO, has described the situation to the consultants in a way that their field interviews reveal isn't accurate. He himself has only the vaguest inkling that his rosy view—his idea that things are in great shape except for a few miscellaneous details—may not be realistic.

Even worse, Kellogg believes that the consultants have created the problems he is just now beginning to see. He doesn't seem to understand that those problems are unavoidable when there is a merger and the leadership fails to provide clear direction or tries to placate both sides.

Given all that, the first thing Susan Barlow should do is pull together some general research and literature about mergers in preparation for the next day's status meeting. It's a safe bet that Kellogg has no experience and no database in this area; few people go through mergers more than once or twice in their careers. Unless Barlow replaces Kellogg's wishful thinking with some informed perspectives, there is relatively little chance that she can help him reevaluate his position and move on to a productive course of action for all the parties.

By doing this research, Barlow, too, will gain some perspective. First, she'll find that mergers are a high-risk undertaking under the best of circumstances. Most studies suggest that less than 50% of mergers ever reach anywhere near the economic or strategic destination that was envisioned for them. In fact, in many cases the mergers fail because the new company's managers underestimated, ignored, or mishandled the integration tasks. In mergers such as Kellogg-Champion, the integration work is especially important. It would be different if Kellogg-Champion were a holding company acquiring a new division in a distinct business, or if it were a new company formed by two organizations that complemented each other by providing links in the supply chain or by offering related goods or services. But for a firm that is formed by two organizations whose customers, products, and markets overlap heavily, the benefits of a merger can be realized only if the new firm can behave as one entity.

There are precious few successful examples of "mergers of equals."

Second, Barlow will learn that there are precious few successful examples of "mergers of equals" in situations in which complete integration is necessary in order to cut costs, release synergy, and blend sales forces and product lines. Usually, success is achieved when one firm's culture and practices dominate. There is some evidence that successful acquirers are typically those organizations with a history of cost control and productivity and, therefore, that the acquirer's culture will be the more successful in directing and getting the most out of the new entity. So an economic Darwinism is at work suggesting that the acquirer's ability to keep acquiring is fostered by a culture and set of practices that have passed substantial market tests and ought to be given preferred status.

Armed with that knowledge, Barlow also will understand—very clearly—that until all the integration issues are resolved, Kellogg-Champion will be too stressed and strained to achieve any new growth or progress. An organization whose employees are dealing with enormous uncertainty as to what the rules are, what the right practices are, and which behaviors are

Barlow should say, "Our firm never should have accepted this assignment, because we can't do it."

approved and which are prohibited will continue to flail against itself like a piece of machinery with badly fitting parts. Not only won't it run well, but it will soon start to eat itself up.

Consider a classic example: the merger of the old Mellon and Gerard banks. Every attempt was made to treat the merger as a joining of equals and not to force common solutions. For several decades, the "old Mellon" and the "old Gerard" really ran as independent fiefdoms, with little interaction and little cooperation, ultimately becoming "Mellon East" and "Mellon West." The lack of leadership probably cost Mellon the opportunity to move early into the ranks of the successful superregional banks. That merger also may have led to some of the company's later moves, which brought the once proud Mellon to the edge of collapse and forced its senior management team to abdicate.

But back to the present. With the Statler Group's assignment structured as it is, Barlow and Roussos are in a no-win situation—both for the client and for themselves. Any attempt to fix it is bound to fail. Therefore, I would advise Barlow to begin her meeting with Kellogg with a strong statement. She should say, "Mr. Kellogg, our firm never should have accepted this assignment, because we can't do it. What needs to be done here is beyond what we or any other consulting firm can do. Fundamental management decisions must be made that cannot be delegated to consultants, regardless of how good they are. We can, and would like, to provide staff and process support to you as a way of helping to get this done, but ultimately these are decisions that you and Mr. Carpenter need to make."

Then if Kellogg hasn't tossed her out on her ear before she has finished speaking, Barlow should review with him some of the research on successful mergers and say something like, "We would recommend that you do one of two things. You can state that the policies of Kellogg & Meyer will be followed unless you or Mr. Carpenter makes an announcement to the contrary. That would, of course, be the fastest way to reduce the uncertainty and get you back to doing business.

"Or—and this second alternative is the one I hope you'll pursue—you can appoint a small group of senior managers from both organizations to review the policies of both former firms and make recommendations to someone with the authority to approve the final policies, organization charts, and so on. That person can be you, Mr. Carpenter, or someone very senior in the firm whom you trust with these decisions, but it must be somebody whose determination will be viewed as final. You and Mr. Carpenter will need to support the decisions. That person should also handle all the communication with employees about the new policies and should ensure that the former employees of both firms are in contact with each other and understand to whom they report and with whom they must work. Clearly, this process would have to be completed with some speed, so that your employees will have a stable climate in which to work."

Finally, Barlow should try to reassure Kellogg that this situation is neither unusual nor a sign that his management team—or the merger—has failed. She might say, "This situation is inevitable when two firms come together, and it takes tremendous effort and high-level involvement and direction to get it done right." She might conclude by telling Kellogg that she and Roussos would be glad to support Kellogg's review team and that, even though the process would take more time than the consultants originally signed on for, they would do the extra work for the fee they had agreed to. She should assure Kellogg that she believes the merger will succeed and that Statler can help it do so.

Obviously, Barlow and Roussos risk being thrown off the account, but this is the only advice they can, in good conscience, give their client. If Kellogg accepts it and they can work with him, they'll have been party to a successful transaction and they also will have improved their chances of winning other accounts in the industry. If he refuses their advice, they should give up the account or allow the assignment to be canceled; they can't afford to stay involved with what is certain to become a public disaster.

CHARLES FOMBRUN *is a professor of management and the director of the Stern Management Consulting Program at New York University's Stern School of Business. He also is the author of* Reputation: Realizing Value from the Corporate Image *(Harvard Business School Press, 1996).*

To put it mildly, Barlow and Roussos completely bungled the Statler Group's initial entry into the client's system: they failed to anticipate their client's concerns about the project's execution; they unquestioningly accepted Kellogg's definition of the engagement without doing any independent fact-finding; and they mishandled Statler's introduction to the rest of the top management team. Not surprisingly, Statler is rapidly losing credibility with everyone at Kellogg-Champion.

It may not be entirely Barlow and Roussos's fault: Statler's client management process is inept across the board. Nevertheless, the two consultants should recognize that they are about to be scapegoated. It will take some skillful maneuvering to salvage the engagement. To maximize their chances, I suggest they do the following:

Prepare for reentry. A critical objective of the status meeting is to create an atmosphere in which Barlow and Roussos can start their work afresh. Right now, Kellogg has serious concerns about their skills; he doubts that they're doing what they're supposed to be doing. Successful reentry depends entirely on demonstrating to a very skeptical Kellogg that Statler is staffed with top-notch consultants at all levels. Rebuilding Kellogg's confidence in Statler's consulting skills is crucial if Barlow and Roussos are to salvage the engagement and their firm's reputation.

That's why Barlow needs to call Statler partner George Gray, explain how the project is unfolding, and ask for his help in straightening out the mess. Under no circumstances should Barlow and Roussos meet with Kellogg on their own. Because the initial contract for the engagement was established with Gray and with a senior consultant whom Barlow subsequently replaced, Gray should be present and fully involved at the status meeting.

Diagnose inaccurate expectations. The status meeting is critical. It will be impossible to reestablish a working relationship until all parties arrive at a convincing diagnosis of the situation. That's why the consultants need to follow a tightly ordered script. I would suggest the following: As the senior partner on the engagement, Gray should open the meeting by reviewing the initial statement of the problem and the agreed-upon objectives. He then should acknowledge his own misunderstanding of how far along toward integration the two firms actually were. The fact is, they are in the very early stages of the process.

The Statler team needs to emphasize the degree of misaligned expectations by both the client and the consultants.

No doubt, after Gray has said his piece, Kellogg will need to vent his anger and frustration. The Statler team should anticipate his concerns and prepare to defuse them—not by ascribing blame to either party but by emphasizing the degree of *misaligned expectations by both the client and the consultants.* To show goodwill, it would be judicious for the Statler Group to offer to write off part or all of the consulting fees that have been accumulated during the last two weeks.

Review the facts. Gray then should reintroduce Barlow and Roussos, building up their experience and expertise, and invite them to summarize the surprising facts they uncovered in their preliminary interviews. Although the consultants actually mishandled the interviews, they should avoid discussing their mistakes. Instead, they should point out that the issues that had been raised by different members of the premerger firms were unexpected and went far beyond a simple combination of policy manuals. Indeed, the feedback hints at some serious unresolved questions about the structure, culture, and strategy of the merged organization. For example, Who will control Kellogg-Champion? Which of the two firms' policies will prevail? and Where is the new firm headed?

Educate the client. Kellogg obviously underestimates the process and content issues involved in completing a merger of two firms that operate in the same industry. The consultants therefore must call on their expertise gained from other merger situations to describe convincingly the necessary steps involved in postmerger integration. It might be useful for Barlow and Roussos to sketch out a typical process and distill the kinds of problems other merged firms have experienced, particularly other securities firms that Kellogg would be familiar with. Unvoiced issues that the consultants also might raise include the competitive implications of a merger of two organizations in the same industry: Will offices be closed, jobs redefined, or employees laid off? How will leadership succession take place? Will some clients be shifted within the merged firm in its efforts to rationalize operations? The Statler team should conclude by presenting a comprehensive model of the strategic, organizational, and operational issues that need to be addressed in order to achieve successful integration.

Reframe the engagement. If the meeting has gone well thus far—that is, if Kellogg has calmed down, is listening, and is back on board—the Statler team should be prepared to present a revised proposal that reframes the engagement and lists a new sequence of steps. Among the first steps that the team should request of Kellogg is a face-to-face meeting of the consultants with the senior managers of both premerger firms. The purpose of the meeting is to introduce the Statler Group properly and explain its role, to develop a common vision of the merged firm, and to endorse a plan for integration. It could turn out to be a long meeting and might be better conducted off-site, preferably in a pastoral setting that would be more conducive to interactive planning.

At this point, even if the Statler consultants work harder than they ever have before, they probably won't salvage the situation. It's a long shot, and they'll need luck on their side. My final word of advice? They should forget the *moo shu* and check out the fortune cookies.

ROBERT H. SCHAFFER *is a principal in the consulting firm Robert H. Schaffer & Associates in Stamford, Connecticut. He also is the author of* High-Impact Consulting: How Clients and Consultants Can Leverage Rapid Results into Long-Term Gains *(Jossey-Bass, 1997). Schaffer has written five articles for HBR.*

One of the most valuable services a consultant can provide is to help clients develop new insights and perspectives about their situations. Unfortunately, even though such fresh understandings almost always lead to more effective action, this kind of help is rarely provided. That is because most consultants see their work as a set of technical tasks aimed at delivering a recommendation or a solution. And that is clearly how Barlow and Roussos viewed their job. They never explored with Kellogg how the amalgamation of policies might contribute to—or interfere with—the specific aims of the merger. Nor did they even try to find out what those aims actually were. Instead, they slipped at once into their well-choreographed study-analyze-recommend routine.

Kellogg, for his part, accepted the consultants' view of their assignment. After all, it was what he wanted to hear. He had told Barlow that "the big integration-related issues had been resolved." The problem is that they were far from resolved. This is Kellogg's first experience with a merger; it appears that he doesn't even have an integration plan. Moreover, his forte is investing, not managing. He may not know what a merger plan should look like or even how to start creating one. My hunch is that the policy amalgamation project was simply a nice, tangible task that Kellogg could launch to reassure himself that he was indeed getting on with the merger.

That's why if Kellogg were to ask me, as a trusted adviser, how he should handle the upcoming meeting, I would suggest he do the following three things:

Clarify what's going on. I would first ask Kellogg to think about what can be learned from what has already taken place. Would he not agree that his associates' reactions in their interviews seemed much too highly charged and intense to have been triggered only by the consultants' techniques? Isn't it logical to suspect that their reactions were, to some extent at least, provoked by tensions that were being aroused by the merger? I would tell Kellogg that such reactions, far from being unusual, are almost inevitable. In every merger, in fact, even the most secure people wonder how they will fare. Will their jobs change? Will their status and security be affected? Since Kellogg hasn't said much about any of those issues, his people's worst fears may have been aroused—even if Kellogg has no intention of firing or demoting a single person. I would suggest to Kellogg that, although he should not be alarmed by his new understanding, he also shouldn't sit still. Which brings me to my next piece of advice:

Use Kellogg-Champion's business goals as the key to formulating a strategy for the merger. Kellogg's overall goal is clearly to be successful in the marketplace with a merger that has gone smoothly. But right now, more attention is being paid to amalgamating policies. True, the policies must be reconciled at some point, but now that project seems to be diverting attention and energy from where they're truly needed.

Kellogg should take a deep breath and think back to why Kellogg & Meyer and Champion Securities made sense as a prospective merger in the first place. Then he should call in his colleagues—indeed, all the senior managers of both former firms—and engage them in the process of identifying Kellogg-Champion's greatest business opportunities. He also should ask for their assistance in designing the plans necessary to exploit those opportunities. Kellogg needs to talk with these people, tell them what he is trying to do, and explain how they will be involved in the work. In other words, he should begin to share accountability with them for the merger's success. If the members of his management team are focused on their new firm's performance, there will be much less anxiety driving them to engage in internal turf battles. Furthermore, when the time comes to tackle the policy amalgamation issues, the process will be easier because all the parties involved can help identify and adapt the approach that best serves their shared vision of Kellogg-Champion's marketplace goals.

I also would suggest that Kellogg tell his management team why he launched the initial consulting assignment and ask for their help in shifting its focus. Up to this point, his people have not had a clear understanding of the consultants' mission. That permitted them to indulge in their wildest fantasies about what the consultants were up to. Once he has had an open discussion with his people, then it's time to deal with the Statler Group. If Kellogg is reasonably confident that he is now on the same page as his senior management team and that everyone is focusing on Kellogg-Champion's business goals, he can:

Test whether the consultants can help. There are two possible ways in which outside consultants can help this merger succeed. One, they can follow through on Kellogg's original idea of a limited assignment: helping to integrate the former organizations' policies when the new firm is ready. Two, they might be able to help formulate and launch an overall strategy for ensuring that the merger is successful.

Can Barlow and Roussos add real value in either of those scenarios? Thus far, they have functioned, as most consultants do, as outsourced technical workers. But a great many people who are trapped in this role would love the opportunity to work in a more advisory mode. Barlow and Roussos may be among them. Kellogg can find out at the status meeting. I would suggest that he ask them some open-ended questions: What is their view of the merged firm's potential in the marketplace? What are its greatest opportunities? Given what they have seen, how can those opportunities be exploited to their fullest? What obstacles have to be overcome? How can that happen? Can policies be merged in a way that helps the firm achieve its business goals? By asking such questions, Kellogg will quickly discover whether the consultants have any relevant capabilities beyond their task-oriented, technical expertise.

Kellogg also will find out whether he wants to continue working with Barlow and Roussos, and if so, whether he wants their role to be large or small, broad or narrow. This, of course, is the kind of exploration that should have shaped the assignment in the first place.

My sense is that the original proposal prepared by the Statler Group was a one-dimensional document that listed the tasks the consultants would perform and the products they would deliver. My final advice to Kellogg, then, is this: If he does decide to continue with the Statler Group, he should try—beginning with the next morning's status meeting—to build the consultant-client relationship on a foundation of mutual understanding of what the two parties are trying to accomplish and of how they will collaborate to make it happen. That's not a guarantee that there won't be more bumps along the path to a truly integrated organization, but it will give him the best shot possible. Mort would have approved.

DAVID H. MAISTER *is a consultant who specializes in professional services firms. He also is the author of* True Professionalism *(The Free Press, 1997).*

It's perhaps understandable that Kellogg thought this was a simple, straightforward assignment, since he seems to have little interest (or experience) in management, or "people stuff." But it's unforgivable that his outside consultants accepted an assignment that was so poorly thought through. They acted very unprofessionally in taking on something that was impossible to do well in the time allowed.

First, there is no such thing as a "merger of equals." In fact, when two companies join forces, it's almost never a merger per se—it's almost always an acquisition. Kellogg's people know this (especially those on the Champion side), his outside consultants should have known it, and someone certainly should have enlightened him. What's more, a merger is never one merger but in fact is made up of tens or hundreds of minimergers, with each department jockeying for power, influence, and authority. Each minimerger needs its own reconciliation process, and many will need third-party facilitation. The consulting team that the Statler Group sent Kellogg— skills or lack thereof aside—is insufficiently staffed to get the job done. Two people are simply inadequate to do what is necessary on this project.

Kellogg shouldn't panic, however. Everything that has happened so far is par for the course in a merger and should have been predicted. But that brings us to what Kellogg needs. What he *doesn't* need is an industry expert like Barlow or a subject matter expert—someone who specializes in compensation or marketing or branch management, for example. He also doesn't need (as he seems to think) a consultant to advise him on administrative processes. Instead, he must find someone who can guide him and his people through the political and interpersonal process of completing the merger. Wanted: a skilled diplomat, a wise counselor, or an organizational tactician who can devise a set of processes to navigate through numerous turf battles.

Kellogg was right about trying to accomplish things quickly. In a merger, there is always a certain amount of pain that must be spread around, and you get one of two choices: either a little pain for a lot of people spread over a long period of time or a lot of pain for a few people in a short period of time. The latter course tends to be the wisest. It's usually better to get things done fast and then move on. Generally, it's ambiguity that distracts people from doing their jobs properly ("How are we going to get paid?") and hurts the organization the most.

However, there's an old saying in the professional services field: The client can have it fast, good, or cheap, but not all three at once. The client gets to pick two out of three. Until now, Kellogg has been going for fast and cheap, and that's not a good choice. He needs fast and good. And that means a consulting team with a different composition from the one he has now.

So where does he go from here? The first thing he should do is get George Gray, the partner who sold him the assignment, on the phone. Kellogg has every right to feel burned by the "bait and switch." Where has Gray been during all of this? Kellogg should insist that Gray be present to hear the report from the two "junior consultants." He needed a high-level political counselor, and he's been given analysts. If Gray can't make it, Kellogg should reschedule the meeting for a time when he can. (Gray will make it—of that I'm sure.)

At the meeting, Kellogg should hear the consultants out and then ask a lot of questions. Among them should be: What do you think the problem is? What do you think is the best process to follow to reconcile the opposing interests of the different groups? Exactly what activities will you engage in? What do you think I should be doing? What help do you need from our employees? How many people would your firm need to provide to do the job right? What would the timeline really look like? How much would that cost?

Kellogg has a number of valid complaints about the consultants, but unless he's prepared to fire them right away, there is no point in dwelling on the critique. He has bigger fish to fry (his merger), and he needs to find out whether Statler's consultants have a revised plan of attack that can help him deal with all his thorny problems.

If they have such a plan, he also needs to know if they can act quickly. Given the hornet's nest the consultants have stirred up (or, at a minimum, surfaced), Kellogg's need for speed is even greater than it was. He probably can buy himself some time by sending out a memo announcing the formation of a merger integration team, preferably staffed with representatives from both Kellogg & Meyer and Champion. But even that team will need to work fast as it treads carefully. Kellogg has been smart to stress balance in the process—that is, being evenhanded in dealing with both sides of the merger. But nothing is more certain to destroy a merger than aiming for balanced results, such as taking equal numbers of policies from both sides or selecting managers equally from both sides. He realizes this; he doesn't want any new policies.

If they are smart, the consultants will themselves recommend that Kellogg form a merger-integration team staffed with his own people, to which they would act as advisers (and to whom they would report). It is often helpful to have consultants around during this process—if only to play the Saint Sebastian role of having the arrows aimed at their flesh—but it's almost certainly a bad idea to give them the whole task to perform. They may know the securities business, but (as is already obvious) they don't know where the land mines are buried. Kellogg also needs to make sure that some members of the integration team have a greater sensitivity to people issues than Kellogg himself has shown. He has, after all, been quite naïve.

It's often said in the professional services world that to do a great job, you have to have a great client. Kellogg has not been a great client. He didn't understand the full scope and challenge of his problems, and he commissioned an approach that was bound to fail. But then, it's also frequently said in consulting circles that the person who hires you is always a part of the problem, and part of great consulting is helping your client understand what that problem is and what is needed to solve it. Kellogg has not been well served.

Originally published in November–December 1997
Reprint 97605

HBR's cases present common managerial dilemmas and offer concrete solutions from experts. As written, they are hypothetical, and the names used are fictitious.

Five Ways to Keep Disputes Out of Court

JOHN R. ALLISON

Executive Summary

EVEN IF YOU WIN, a lawsuit can be a disaster. Attorney fees eat up $20 billion a year in the United States alone, and that doesn't count the cost of diverting key personnel from productive work or of damaging profitable business relationships. But more and more managers are discovering that litigation can be avoided with inventive use of alternative dispute resolution, or ADR.

All forms of ADR are designed to do two things; save time and money and soften the sharp edges of the adversarial system. In the majority of cases, disputants settle their differences quickly and to the satisfaction of both parties. In the best of cases, opponents resolve their disputes cooperatively and forge new ties.

Arbitration, the oldest and most adversarial form of ADR, is now the compulsory prerequisite to litigation in about 20 states. *Mediation*, perhaps the most versatile and the least coercive, depends greatly on the skill and personality of the mediator. Other methods include the *rent-a-judge program, summary jury trial,* and *minitrial,* all of which simulate real litigation to one degree or another but with greater speed, more privacy, and less expense. (The last two have settled several bitter disputes in weeks—after years of litigation.) Variations and hybrids of ADR methods are limitless.

In picking the ADR method best suited to your circumstances, factors to consider include: the extent to which both disputants are committed to ADR, the closeness of the business relationship between the two parties, the need for privacy, the urgency of reaching a settlement, the absolute and the relative financial health of both parties, the importance of the principles involved, the complexity of the case, the size of the stakes, and the ability and willingness of company executives to get involved.

T HERE ARE FEW THINGS managers dread more than litigation. Even petty cases have a way of damaging relationships, tarnishing reputations, and eating up enormous sums of money, time, and talent. Most managers know that lawsuits are steadily increasing. Smart managers know that they are also increasingly avoidable. There are now many alternatives to litigation that can nip lawsuits in the bud, resolve long-standing disputes, and even produce win-win solutions to old and bitter fights that would otherwise only leave both sides damaged.

U.S. corporations pay more than $20 billion a year to litigation attorneys—an alarming fact that distracts our attention from other and often more important business costs of litigating our disputes. Lawyers' fees and other direct costs get the most attention because they're easy to measure. But the indirect business costs of litigation, the cost of diverting key personnel from productive activities, for example, or the cost of destroying a profitable relationship with a former business ally, are perhaps equally important. From the company's perspective, they may be *more* important.

The high cost of resolving disputes has several causes, but the most important is the mind-set established and nurtured by the adversary system. The essence of this system is that lawyers for opposing parties have the responsibility to present every piece of evidence and make every legal argument that might possibly benefit their clients. Pretrial discovery and other litigation procedures are designed to leave no stone unturned in the search for relevant evidence. By training, temperament, professional duty, and frequently by client expectation, attorneys tend to exploit these procedures to the fullest and to persevere as long as any hope remains. In fact, each lawyer has an obligation to be as zealous an advocate as possible, even—sometimes especially—to the detriment of discovering the truth and of resolving conflicts to the *satisfaction* of both parties.

The idea behind the adversary system is that the truth will emerge when opposing sides present their cases as aggressively as possible. Even though this ideal is not always realized, the principle is probably sound. The problem with the adversary method in civil cases is not theoretical but practical. First, it is not the most effective way to resolve some kinds of disputes. Second, it can be made more effective for most kinds of disputes by borrowing certain of the nonadversarial features of other forms of dispute resolution. Third, from both the societal and the individual perspective, we may no longer be able to afford it in its undiluted form. (See "The Jury Is Still Out on the U.S. Civil Justice System" at the end of this article.)

Alternatives to traditional litigation have been around for many years, but Alternative Dispute Resolution (ADR) as a formal technique and an accepted business practice emerged in the 1970s.

The ADR Mind-Set

Judge Dorothy Nelson of the U.S. Court of Appeals in San Francisco traveled to Israel several years ago to study the laws of divorce as administered by different religious groups. In Jerusalem she attended a court hearing conducted by three Greek Orthodox priests in long black robes and long white beards. Court was conducted in a Quonset hut with paint peeling from the walls, furnished only with a plain wooden table and chairs. A wife was suing her husband for divorce. As her lawyer rose to his feet holding a handful of papers from which to plead her case, he was waived gently aside by the presiding priest, who turned to the wife and asked her to tell her own story.

She explained that for five years of marriage she had shared a house with her mother-in-law. The older woman, too old to climb stairs, occupied the ground floor, and the wife lived upstairs. Since there was only one entrance to the house, she had to enter through her mother-in-law's living quarters to get to her own, and her mother-in-law continually questioned her about her activities and offered unsolicited advice. She loved her husband, she said, but the situation was intolerable.

The wife sat down and the presiding priest, waiving aside the husband's lawyer as he had the wife's, asked to hear the husband's side of the case. The husband said that he loved his wife but also his mother. As a Christian he felt responsibility for both, but he was a poor man and could not afford two households.

The three priests retired by stepping into the dusty street outside and returned five minutes later with their judgment. The husband was to purchase a ladder. When the wife wanted to avoid her mother-in-law, she could climb the ladder directly to her second-floor window.

Judge Nelson says that as she watched husband and wife leave the Quonset hut hand in hand, she could only wonder what might have happened to this couple under an adversary system, with its orders to show cause, its lengthy hearings, and its high attorney fees.

The modern American manager must operate within just such an adversarial legal system, with all its complications and formalities. And yet there may be more similarities between the Middle Eastern marital dispute and the American business dispute than one might think. Long-term business relationships can be as valuable to a company as long-term personal relationships to people's lives. The rupture of either can be devastating. Moreover, in either situation, the resolution process itself can take a heavy toll on the participants if creative methods of resolving disputes are not given a chance. Perhaps the most important parallel, however, is that the modern manager can follow the lead of the priests in seeking a better way.

To most people, ADR means any method of resolving disputes other than litigation, which is correct only if litigation includes not only cases that actually go to trial but also lawsuits that are settled before they get to court. This point is important for two reasons. First, more than 90% of all lawsuits are settled out of court, most of them virtually on the courthouse steps after months or years of preparation and expense. Some of this expense is necessary, but, on the whole, huge quantities of time and money are spent preparing for events that don't occur. Second, the very initiation of a lawsuit, even if it is settled prior to trial, gives rise to the adversarial mindset, which then makes its own prodigious contribution to cost, delay, and acrimony.

As we will see, some ADR mechanisms work better than others in any given case. But all share two characteristics: they are all attempts to save legal and managerial time and money, and they all try to take at least some of the edge off the adversarial attitude. The theory behind ADR is that settling disputes as painlessly as possible requires good communication, that good communication requires some degree of trust, and that the adversary system of dispute resolution nurtures distrust, distortion, and animosity. The creation of trust is central to the design of many ADR techniques.

The ADR Menu

The manager of today has available an array of ADR methods that were unheard of a few years ago. For these alternatives to be of much use, however, the manager must know something about how they work, why they exist, and what they can and cannot achieve. If nothing else, a familiarity with ADR methods may cause a manager to think seriously about dispute resolution at an earlier stage of any disagreement.

Dispute resolution—litigation or ADR—is not an activity that thrives in a little black box. At its best, it is a joint venture between the company and its attorneys, requiring management participation as early and completely as possible. Handled with sufficient skill, ADR can bring an opponent into the venture as well, as all parties join in a nonadversarial search for a mutually beneficial outcome.

The most common forms of ADR are arbitration, mediation, the rent-a-judge program, summary jury trial, and minitrial, although techniques can be combined to form hybrids suited to a particular dispute or legal jurisdiction.

Arbitration, which is basically adversarial in nature and produces a binding decision made by a third party, is the form of ADR that most resembles litigation.

The decision to seek arbitration is sometimes made after a conflict has arisen, but much more often the parties have a clause in their contract committing them to arbitration of disputes arising from their business together. In labor relations, arbitration agreements are usually included as the capstone of the grievance procedures specified in the collective bargaining contract.

In theory, arbitration rules are up to the disputants to decide, but in practice most adopt the procedures recommended by the American Arbitration Association (AAA). In essence, the parties to the dispute choose either a single arbitrator or a panel of arbitrators (usually three), who then hear evidence and arguments from attorneys and render a legally binding decision.

In the case of interstate or foreign commerce, the United States Arbitration Act of 1925 makes the agreement legally enforceable, and most states have similar laws for agreements not covered by the federal statute. If asked to review a decision, a court can hear complaints only about fundamental procedural fairness or the arbitrator's conduct, not about the merits of the case.

(Though the Taft-Hartley Act provides a separate legal framework for the enforcement of labor arbitration agreements, commercial and labor arbitration are in fact quite similar in both law and practice. The main difference is that labor arbitration is more institutionalized and so a bit more formal. Another distinction is that labor arbitrators are customarily paid, whereas those in domestic commercial arbitration are not usually compensated unless the proceeding is unusually lengthy.)

Despite its superficial resemblance to litigation, however, commercial arbitration is truly an alternative mechanism. Under AAA guidelines, parties to a dispute can still make some important exceptions to the rules. For example, arbitrators are not required to have a legal background or even to follow the formal rules of law or evidence unless the disputants so stipulate. And there is seldom any period of prehearing discovery. In general, arbitration is much less formal than litigation and requires much less time and money.

Although commercial arbitration has traditionally been purely a creature of mutual consent, one feature of the modern ADR movement has been the development in about 20 states and 10 federal district courts of compulsory but nonbinding arbitration as a prerequisite to litigation.

Mediation differs greatly from arbitration in that the neutral third party, the mediator, does not impose a solution. The object of mediation is to help the parties resolve their own dispute, so a mediator's functions can vary depending on the personalities and wishes of the parties and their attorneys, the nature and history of the dispute, and the personality and skills of the mediator.

Arranged in order from the least to the most active, a list of the mediator's many different jobs and roles can read almost like a diary. In the course of an actual mediation, a good mediator might do every one of the following things, in roughly the following order: urge participants to talk to each other; help them to understand the nature and objectives of mediation; carry messages; help the parties agree on an agenda, or, failing that, set an agenda; provide a suitable environment for negotiation; maintain order; help disputants understand their problems and the source of their conflict; defuse unrealistic expectations; help participants develop their own proposals; help them negotiate; suggest solutions; and, finally, persuade them to accept a specific resolution.

Mediation has been used to settle conflicts of every kind, from international political disagreements and labor disputes to landlord-tenant, consumer, and medical malpractice contests. There has been a rapid increase in business use of mediation over the past few years, some of it in imaginative new forms.

In 1982, IBM claimed that Fujitsu had illegally copied IBM's mainframe operating system software. The two reached a settlement in 1983, but further disputes continued to break out, in large part because of the technological complexity and legal uncertainty of many of the issues. In 1985, IBM demanded arbitration as provided for in the 1983 accord. Two arbitrators were chosen as a panel, one a law professor experienced in dispute resolution and the other a retired computer industry executive. The arbitrators quickly saw that without some innovative thinking the proceeding was going to bog down in the same morass of technical detail and fingerpointing that blocked the resolution negotiated earlier. They refused to hear more specific complaints. Instead they issued an order compelling Fujitsu to provide a complete accounting of its use of programs covered by the 1983 accord and requiring the two companies to participate in a mediation procedure covering programs not included in the earlier agreement.

The arbitrators then became the mediators and negotiated two new agreements, one resolving almost all of the past-use issues and the other governing future relations. Then the panel switched roles once again by incorporating the agreements into a binding arbitration decision. Fujitsu purchased a retroactive license for the use of designated programs, and IBM dropped its copyright infringement claims. For the future, each company was required to license its operating systems for use on the other company's hardware whenever customers requested it. The amount of compensation, the duration of the arrangement, and other specific issues were left for binding arbitration as they arose. Although this creative use of mediation was to some extent forced on the disputants, it wouldn't have worked had the parties not made a good faith commitment to ADR and, specifically, to mediation, once the artibrators had ordered it.

The rent-a-judge program is a novel variant of arbitration where the parties to the dispute choose a retired judge to hear their case much as an arbitrator would. Retired judges are occasionally used in traditional arbitration too, but the rent-a-judge program uses normal trial court procedures (sometimes modified by the disputants). Moreover, the judge's decision has, by statute, the legal status of a real court judgment. The experiment has enjoyed a significant measure of success and acceptance in the jurisdictions where it has been authorized, notably California, but it's too early to tell how widespread it will become. Since it isn't necessary to wait for a court date or to conduct the proceedings in public, the program buys a lot of time and privacy. However, some observers are uneasy about starting down a road that might lead to a formally sanctioned class of justice available only to those who can pay for it.

Summary jury trial is based on the observation that litigants are often unable to settle their disputes quickly because of the huge gap in their differing expectations of how a jury will view their claims. To overcome this impasse and give disputants a nonbinding indication of how their claims might actually be received, federal district judge Thomas Lambros invented the summary jury trial, or SJT, in his Cleveland courtroom in 1983, and, with a few variations here and there, the procedure has since found its way into many other federal and state courts.

The process works like this: opposing lawyers select a small jury, usually six members, from the regular jury pool. (To ensure that the jury will take its responsibility seriously, most judges do not tell jurors beforehand that their verdict will be advisory only.) The judge gives the jury preliminary instructions on the law, the lawyers make short opening statements, then each side has a limited time, typically an hour, to summarize the evidence it would otherwise present at a trial. Following brief rebuttals, the lawyers present closing arguments in which they interpret and characterize the evidence they have previously described. The judge charges the jury, gives it final instructions on the law, and the jury retires to reach its verdict.

The disputants themselves, or, in the case of a corporation, an executive with settlement authority, must attend the entire proceeding, which normally lasts one day but occasionally two. Immediately after the verdict, the disputants are sent to a settlement negotiation, usually without their attorneys. If no settlement is reached, neither the occurrence nor the result of the SJT is admissible when the case later goes to court.

About 95% of all cases are settled relatively quickly after the jury's verdict. Evidence to date suggests that the courts that use SJT shave substantial time off their aggregate case-processing time. Federal district judge S. Arthur Spiegel estimated, for example, that in just over a year in his Ohio courtroom, eight SJTs saved more than 100 days of actual trial time. Of course, it is very hard to say whether the parties to any given dispute save time and money because the comparison is between what actually happened with SJT and what might have happened without it. But judges claim that they choose cases for SJT that have a less than average chance of settlement and that suggest considerable savings for winner and loser as well.

Although SJT has had several important successes, including settlement of a difficult $2.5 million antitrust case in Judge Lambros's court, praise for SJT is not unanimous. Some question the ethics of not telling the jury in advance that its verdict is merely advisory, although doing otherwise runs a big risk of lessening jurors' commitment to the task. Others are concerned that overall community commitment to jury service may decline as more and more jurors discover, and tell their friends, that juries don't necessarily have any authority.

Another danger is that in some cases SJT actually decreases the odds of settlement when the defendant wins. As a result, some courts ask juries for several verdicts. First, who wins? Second, if the plaintiff wins, what are the damages? Third, if the defendant wins, what does the jury believe the plaintiff's damages should have been if the plaintiff had won? This kind of multiple verdict, however confusing and hypothetical, provides more information on which to base the ensuing settlement talks and helps avoid the all-or-nothing attitude that can so easily encumber any adversarial negotiation.

Minitrial is a hybrid of mediation, traditional settlement negotiation, and adjudication. It is a completely voluntary procedure normally initiated by the disputants themselves, although judges may suggest or encourage it where suit has already been filed.

Minitrial formats vary somewhat but typically involve one high-level executive from each side of the dispute plus one neutral adviser, sometimes a former judge but often a nonjudicial expert in the subject matter of the contest. To minimize the role of emotion and face saving, the two executives should not have been directly involved in creating or in trying to settle the case, and they must have either settlement authority or, at the very least, substantial influence over the settlement decision.

Prior to minitrial, the parties informally exchange key documents, exhibits, short briefs, and summaries of witnesses' testimony. They also reach agreement on format, timing, and procedures, and they may even engage in very abbreviated discovery and take short depositions from some of the key witnesses. The whole process usually takes from one to four days.

At the hearing, each side uses its allotted time to present its best case to the neutral observer and the two executives. Presentations often consist primarily of descriptive summaries of evidence but may include visual aids, exhibits, and brief testimony from lay or expert witnesses. During the presentations, or in a separate session at the end, the three observers are free to ask questions and explore the strengths and weaknesses of each case. At the hearing's conclusion, the executives may seek the neutral adviser's opinion about a likely trial outcome before they begin settlement talks, or they may solicit their advice only if they fail to settle on their own.

One well-known case of a successful minitrial involved Allied Corporation and Shell Oil. After five or six years of bickering over a contract dispute, Shell finally filed suit. Four years later, legal fees had consumed hundreds of thousands of dollars and pretrial discovery was not yet complete. Attorneys for both companies decided to use the minitrial in a final effort to resolve the case without a trial. After a short hearing, the parties settled the ten-year-old dispute almost at once. We can only guess how much time, money, and grief might have been avoided by attempting a minitrial years earlier.

Variations and hybrids of the methods outlined here can take an infinite variety of forms, depending on the ingenuity of disputants, attorneys, judges, and even legislators. In some jurisdictions, legislators have mandated prescreening of medical malpractice cases by a panel with balanced representation of doctors, attorneys, and laypeople. Other possible hybrids might include combinations of mediation and case evaluation by a panel of neutral attorneys, blends of mediation and arbitration like the one in the IBM-Fujitsu case, and mixed fact-finding and conciliation performed by a court-appointed expert.

ADR does not always work. But when it fails to produce an acceptable resolution, management can comfort itself with the fact that the effort has not been wasted. Most of the time and money already spent on the unsuccessful ADR procedure will be useful in preparing for trial.

Making the Choice

In the past, decisions about the use of ADR were often spontaneous or ad hoc, but corporate leadership can now

formulate a company ADR policy and analyze each situation to find an effective ADR method—or reject them all
in favor of the courts. (See "Getting Started with ADR" at
the end of this article.) Aetna Life Insurance, among
others, now actively seeks ADR solutions to all its disputes except those involving policyholder claims. Since
no single ADR method is necessarily best, and since
sometimes no ADR method will work, choices about ADR
should take into account at least the following factors:

Commitment. The chances of success for any kind of
ADR are pretty slim unless both parties are committed
to the idea and willing to act in good faith. A disputant
who is dishonest, intractable, or suspicious of any procedure short of litigation is not a promising candidate for
ADR. (The one method that can sometimes succeed even
when one party is opposed to ADR is mediation, for the
very good reason that in mediation the disputants retain
control of a basically informal process requiring no prior
commitment to the outcome.)

A company's lawyers must also be committed to ADR.
At the very least, attorneys must be willing and able to
set aside their predisposition against ADR when the
client wants to use it, but genuine commitment is preferable. It is clearly in a company's best interests to have the
advice of open-minded outside and in-house counsel
when putting together an ADR policy or when exploring
the use of ADR in an individual dispute. In fact, for companies with frequent disputes to settle, it may be a good
idea to have an ADR expert in the general counsel's
office. This person can educate corporate personnel and
perhaps outside lawyers about ADR, formulate corporate
ADR policy, draft and oversee ADR provisions in the
company's contracts, supervise and coordinate the ADR

process in particular cases, and even serve as a devil's advocate in testing the soundness of proposed litigation.

Developing a comprehensive dispute resolution plan is worth time and attention for companies that are large enough or that are in contentious kinds of businesses (construction, say, or insurance). Some companies—ITT, for example—try to include clauses in all their contracts committing all parties involved to some form of ADR.

Relationship. ADR is very good at settling disputes between companies with mutually advantageous relationships that both parties want to maintain. Conversely, disputes arising from one-shot transactions between parties with no expected future together are harder to resolve out of court. Litigation usually produces enough acrimony to rupture the most profitable relationship. Even the most adversarial of ADR techniques, arbitration, is significantly less likely to destroy commercial bonds because of its informality and privacy.

Privacy. Although judges can issue protective orders covering legally qualified trade secrets, much valuable proprietary information cannot be protected in a trial. Moreover, any hearing in a public forum can lead to embarrassing revelations of business and personal behavior, with predictable and not-so-predictable adverse effects on customers, suppliers, shareholders, employees, news media, and even legislative and regulatory bodies.

Direct negotiation clearly offers the most privacy because it does not involve third parties. Failing that, arbitration is generally considered the most private form of resolution because the arbitrator's code of ethics demands complete confidentiality. Moreover, the privacy value of all ADR techniques can be increased by writing confidentiality obligations into contracts.

Urgency. Many disputes need to be settled quickly. A patent or trade-secret struggle could easily cast an intolerable pall over new product development, for example, or a trademark battle might hold up critical marketing plans. For that matter, a new or beleaguered management team might simply need to resolve a dispute quickly for the sake of appearances.

In the relatively rare case where two parties find themselves in basic agreement about the facts and disagree only about the law, summary judgment in a lawsuit may actually be the quickest way to settle. But the traditional forms of adversarial negotiation and litigation usually don't meet anyone's need for a quick resolution. Mediation often provides the fastest fix because it is completely under the disputants' control. Minitrials can also be fast, but they work best when preceded by at least a short period of discovery. The same is true of summary jury trial, but so far parties usually have resorted to SJT only after a lawsuit has already consumed a good deal of time and energy. Arbitration can be very fast if the lawyers on both sides want it to be, but disputants cannot completely control the speed of the process because they have to work with an independent arbitrator and within a sponsoring organization's (like the AAA's) administrative requirements.

Finances. Both the absolute and the relative financial positions of disputing parties are sometimes relevant. A plaintiff's precarious financial condition can increase its need for a fast resolution but can also cause it to hold out to the very end for a potentially large jury verdict.

The course it chooses will depend on how it perceives the strength of its claim but also on just how hard its creditors are breathing down its neck. A financially strapped defendant is likely to benefit from delay if it sees real strength in the other side's claim, especially if applicable law does not provide for prejudgment interest on the court's award.

Large differences in the financial resources of opposing companies can sometimes have perverse effects on settlement efforts. The weaker party may want the protection of a formal court proceeding and be less likely to trust ADR. A court-supervised method such as SJT can reduce this kind of nervousness, as can the involvement of a sponsoring arbitration organization and an authoritative arbitrator.

Although the charge is practically impossible to document, some observers feel that any form of non-court-supervised ADR is likely to be unfair when one party has a great resource advantage over the other. They argue that voluntary ADR rests on agreement rather than decree, and in reaching agreement the smaller, weaker party always suffers some sense of intimidation, however subtle, regardless of the merits of its case. A large corporation proposing ADR to a smaller adversary should be prepared to counter this argument.

Principle.   In some cases, the desire to clear a reputation or defend a principle can be powerful. A corporation is charged with fraud or some other offense tinged with immorality. A manager with a strong sense of innocence is charged with sexual harassment. An individual's insurance claim is denied on suspicion of arson. Private, informal means of resolution, like mediation or even minitrial, may not meet the need for personal vindication. Short of a fullblown trial, the only acceptable procedures are likely to be SJT or arbitration because they let both sides tell their stories to an impartial referee, who then delivers a clear-cut pronouncement of guilt or exoneration.

Principle can also play a role when one or both parties need a legal precedent. A company whose business generates disputes involving questions governed by murky or conflicting points of law may need to win a couple of lawsuits.

Complexity. Some experts will disagree, but I believe that ADR has its greatest potential for saving time and money in complex cases. Complexity comes in different shapes and sizes, of course—factual, legal, multiparty, and various combinations of the three. The minitrial works well in cases of factual and legal complexity but doesn't seem to lend itself well to multiparty disputes. Mediation is suited to all kinds of complexity and may be the best form of ADR for multiparty cases.

Some observers claim that SJT is not well suited to highly complex cases because it requires more jury education than the procedure can accommodate. Yet in June 1989, SJT led to the successful resolution of a $300 million class action suit against National Lead Company and the Department of Energy by a group of 14,000 plaintiffs in a case involving the release of uranium waste into the atmosphere in Fernald, Ohio. Due to the complexity of the case, the SJT took ten days instead of the customary one or two, but litigation and appeals could have dragged on for months or years. The summary jury returned a verdict of $136 million, including punitive damages, and the two sides settled a short time later for $73 million, despite the fact that earlier settlement negotiations had reached a complete impasse.

Most important, both sides felt vindicated by the outcome. The plaintiffs' sense of outrage was assuaged by the finding of culpability, and their fears of health effects were lessened by a medical monitoring program, while the defendants felt that the jury's finding of only $1 million in property damage affirmed their contention that no one had been hurt.

Stakes. No type of ADR is inherently limited in terms of the dollar size of the disputes it can resolve, but some disputants may feel that big-ticket cases belong in a court, with its procedural protections and rights of appeal. As with complex cases, however, big-ticket cases offer a superb opportunity for huge savings in direct and indirect litigation costs.

Of course, even large litigation costs may seem paltry by comparison with a really outrageous claim, or (depending on your point of view) a truly princely award. Nevertheless, various forms of ADR have led to negotiated—and presumably mutually acceptable—settlements of a $200 million fight involving a hospital construction project, a $60 million claim for breach of a contract for the use of municipal garbage as boiler fuel, and a $28 million cost-overrun claim in an oil tanker construction deal.

Executive involvement. People commonly view dispute resolution as a lawyer's problem, for lawyers to work out behind closed doors with little supervision. To be sure, traditional litigation offers few opportunities for close involvement by individual managers. But in any form of ADR, early and personal involvement by the disputants themselves or by the executives of quarreling corporations is often critical to an efficient, expeditious resolution. By their very nature, ADR mechanisms require greater participation by the disputing parties and respond to it more positively. A manager's investment of time and effort will generate excellent returns in the long run.

For those who nevertheless want to keep their distance, arbitration probably works best and mediation worst. SJT and the minitrial may work reasonably well too because both function best when managers with no previous involvement in the dispute represent the two parties.

One of the best things about ADR is that it presents opportunities for managers and lawyers to be creative. Litigation and most adversarial settlement negotiations are based solely on legalistic evaluation in dollar terms. With the active involvement of management, ADR makes it easier to view dispute resolution as a business problem and to investigate business solutions.

Texaco and Borden, for example, were locked in a lawsuit involving a $200 million antitrust and breach-of-contract claim. After several years of legal maneuvering, with about a third of the pretrial discovery process completed and half a million documents already assembled, both counsels decided to attempt a minitrial. Stunningly, the case was settled in three weeks.

The process got off to a good start. Both companies appointed executive vice presidents with wide authority as their minitrial representatives, so each side knew the other was serious about finding a solution. Next, the companies and their lawyers developed the actual format in about an hour, with simple rules: lawyers for each party made extremely abbreviated presentations to the two VPs, who had the help of senior executives and financial experts as technical advisers.

The hearing went smoothly, and over the next two weeks, despite an early impasse, the VPs reached an agreement that both parties described as "win-win." No money changed hands. Instead, the companies renegotiated another gas supply contract that had not been at issue in the case, creating a new arrangement for conveying Texaco gas to Borden.

By giving the disputants their first balanced view of the dispute, the minitrial catalyzed a creative solution that focused almost completely on *business* objectives. It is hard to believe that a judicial resolution could possibly have worked as well. The minitrial dramatically reduced the length of the dispute, slashed legal fees, and plugged the drain on corporate productivity.

In the Texaco-Borden and IBM-Fujitsu disputes, as well as in many other cases of notable ADR success, participating executives and attorneys agreed that trust building and commitment to the idea of avoiding further acrimony were crucial. There is a similar consensus about the necessity of building an ADR knowledge base within the corporation. In most of the early uses of ADR, managers and lawyers acquired this knowledge in the course of experimental use of ADR techniques. A more systematic and comprehensive anticipatory study of ADR outside a case-specific context should become part of every manager's agenda.

Getting Started with ADR

IF IT LOOKS LIKE ADR might be worth a try, it is probably a good idea to go slowly. Experiment with a case in which there is little to lose. One expert even suggests starting with a dispute that looks like a certain loser.

Once management is completely sold on ADR, many proponents suggest that the company develop a formal dispute resolution policy containing elements like these:

Dispute Prevention

- A compliance program for the areas of greatest legal risk, such as employment discrimination, minimum wage and overtime, antitrust, and environmental protection.
- A system to monitor contract performance by both parties.
- A formal policy for identifying potential disputants, handling their inquiries and complaints as early and sensitively as possible, and encouraging dialogue with them. IBM's Corporate Ambassador or Control Data's Ombudsman program might serve as examples.

Dispute Resolution

- A system of litigation risk analysis to determine probabilities of litigation and to estimate the dollar values of actual and potential legal problems.
- A matrix, decision tree, or other multifactor analytical framework for deciding whether litigation or ADR is most appropriate for resolving any given dispute and which form of ADR is most appropriate.

Dispute Management

- A framework to develop and monitor a budget for resolving each dispute, regardless of resolution method. Often the most expensive element of direct litigation is attorneys' fees. If less attorney time is spent on ADR than on litigation, which certainly ought to be the case, management must make sure that the savings are passed on to the company. If this isn't happening, serious fee discussions should take place.
- An aggregate dispute managment system for coordinating, tracking, and troubleshooting all current disputes.

The Jury Is Still Out on the U.S. Civil Justice System

ACCORDING TO ITS MANY detractors, the civil justice system in the United States is a catastrophe. Americans, they argue, are too litigious, given to filing lawsuits almost as a reflex action in response to any perceived wrong. Juries are too susceptible to attorneys' tricks and too likely to reach irrational verdicts against defendants with deep pockets. Lawyers are too greedy. As the principal beneficiaries of the system, they encourage unnecessary litigation and do their best to protect the status quo.

The system also has its defenders. They argue that we most certainly are not, and would not want to be, a passive people, accepting wrongs with fatalistic resignation. Most of us, they say, are deeply committed to the rule of law in our public and private dealings and to the idea that those who violate this rule should be held accountable. Moreover, our society is relatively well educated and doubtless the most diverse and open the world has ever known. Admittedly, these factors translate into a heavy utilization of the courts, but they also translate into features of American life that are highly desirable, not least among them our jealous guardianship of individual freedoms and the democratic ideal.

The system's defenders also argue that because our legal profession is better educated, more heterogeneous, and more richly rewarded than in many other societies, it is more in tune with the value we place on the rule of law and therefore a better buffer against tyranny.

Whatever the truth of these arguments, the U.S. legal system does have some rather obvious and painful shortcomings. There *are* too many lawsuits—the case load is in danger of strangling the courts—and they *do* cost too much. Many frivolous claims are not screened out early enough. We do a poor job of handling worthy small claims. Although the use of juries in civil cases does have some definite merits (providing continuous citizen input into the definition of community values, for example, and serving as a limited check on the judicial branch of government), it also contributes to the system's perceived faults. Juries probably misunderstand issues more often than we would like to admit. They are certainly more susceptible to courtroom histrionics than are judges or other trained and experienced decision makers. And many rules of procedure and evidence that lengthen and complicate lawsuits exist solely to accommodate an untrained and inexperienced fact-finding body.

While most courts have experienced dramatic increases in filings during the past two decades, the problems of civil justice in the United States have more to do with quality than quantity. Given the size and complexity of our society, and the value we place on protecting rights, it is at least plausible to view the number of lawsuits as a natural and unalarming phenomenon. The more important questions are qualitative: Does our legal system give us value? Are the costs and delays commensurate with the level of satisfaction we experience? Does the system resolve disputes—or does it offer only conflict, with no one really winning in the end?

Originally published in January–February 1990
Reprint 90101

Alternative Dispute Resolution

Why It Doesn't Work and
Why It Does

TODD B. CARVER AND

ALBERT A. VONDRA

Executive Summary

IN THE 1980S, experts and executives alike heralded alternative dispute resolution as a sensible, cost-effective way to keep corporations out of court and away from the kind of litigation that devastates winners almost as much as losers. But the great hopes for ADR faded quickly. Damage awards, legal billings, and the number of lawsuits in the Unites States continued to rise—even for many of the companies that had embraced ADR.

What had gone wrong? Was ADR just an empty promise? The authors found that the problem was not with ADR itself, but with ADR as currently practiced by many companies. Indeed, ADR procedures often include so much excess baggage—motions, briefs, discovery, depositions, judges, lawyers—that the entire process can end up costing as much as the litigation it's supposed to prevent. What characterizes ineffective ADR? An emphasis on winning at any price, a lack of commitment to ADR on the part of both top-level management and company counsel, and the misconception that ADR is not really that different from litigation.

But some companies are using ADR effectively—lowering costs, resolving disputes rapidly, and preserving business relationships. Few companies have made the commitment to ADR more effectively than NCR. In addition to boosting the commitment of top management to ADR, NCR has defined a number of goals to be pursued in the event of a dispute. Goals like streamlining the proceedings help ensure that arbitration will really be arbitration and not litigation-in-disguise. Finally, the company has created a systematic process, called the Dispute Avoidance Resolution Process, that mandates ADR as the first step in every legal action.

BACK IN THE 1980S, experts and executives alike heralded alternative dispute resolution (ADR) as a sensible, cost-effective way to keep corporations out of court and away from the kind of litigation that devastates winners almost as much as losers. Over the next few years, more than 600 large corporations adopted the ADR policy statement suggested by the Center for Public Resources, and many of these companies reported considerable savings in time and money. (See "Alternatives to Litigation" and "The Center for Public Resources Policy Statement" at the end of this article.)

But the great hopes for ADR faded quickly. Damage awards, legal billings, and the number of lawsuits in the United States continued to rise—even for many of the companies that had embraced ADR. In fact, one study found that rather than reducing costs and delays, at least one form of ADR—court-annexed arbitration—had actually increased them.

What had gone wrong? Was ADR really just an empty promise? We believed it was not, but lack of success with ADR at so many companies prompted us to take a closer look at how managers were implementing the ADR process.

We found bad news and good. The bad news is that ADR as currently practiced too often mutates into a private judicial system that looks and costs like the litigation it's supposed to prevent. At many companies, ADR procedures now typically include a lot of excess baggage in the form of motions, briefs, discovery, depositions, judges, lawyers, court reporters, expert witnesses, publicity, and damage awards beyond reason (and beyond contractual limits).

The good news is that a number of companies have learned to use ADR effectively, and those companies are in fact reaping ADR's predicted benefits: lower costs, quicker dispute resolutions, and outcomes that preserve and sometimes even improve relationships.

At Chevron, for instance, ADR-based mediation of one dispute cost $25,000, whereas mediation through outside counsel would have cost an estimated $700,000 and going to court as much as $2.5 million over a period of three to five years. At Toyota's U.S. subsidiary, a Reversal Arbitration Board, set up to ease contention between the company and its dealers concerning allocation of cars and sales credits, has brought about a steady decline in the number of these cases, from 178 cases in 1985 to 3 in 1992.

What are Chevron and Toyota doing that other companies are not? The difference between success and failure lies chiefly in the level of commitment. Companies that give ADR top priority—even in cases where they're *sure* they're right—are realizing immense savings of time, money, and relationships. In contrast, companies that let old litigious habits worm their way into the process might as well go back to court.

Few companies have made the commitment to ADR more effectively than NCR (recently renamed AT&T Global Information Solutions). NCR executives made a firm commitment to alternative dispute resolution a decade ago, and the results have been dramatic: the number of the company's filed lawsuits (excluding insured risks) pending in the United States dropped from 263 in March 1984 to 28 in November 1993. Last year, only nine disputes incurred outside attorneys' fees exceeding $20,000, and total outside legal fees—not quite $1 million—were less than half what they were in 1984. Moreover, the reduction in outside fees has not increased the costs of in-house counsel. NCR manages its filed cases with only four in-house lawyers and four paralegals.

Several years ago, in a case in which it did not have an arbitration clause, NCR spent hundreds of thousands of dollars defending itself in a conventional lawsuit and nevertheless lost a multimillion-dollar jury verdict. In the past five years, NCR has paid out less in awards and settlements—and in outside and in-house counsel fees for all of its ADR matters—than the outlays for that single case.

How ADR Goes Wrong

As we've said, to make alternative dispute resolution work, management must adopt the principle wholeheartedly. Consider the following sad but true story of two large electronics manufacturers—both, ironically, subscribers to the Center for Public Resources policy statement.

About 15 years ago, Company A, which makes computer-support products, licensed Company B to manufacture a new device. The arrangement was a means of expanding the market by offering a second source of the product. The device was wildly successful, but by the mid-1980s, Company A had developed its technology and improved the device, and it refused to let Company B manufacture the new design. Fearing it would lose a lucrative market, Company B threatened a lawsuit, and when the threat had no effect, it reverse engineered the new device and began to manufacture and market its own version. Now it was Company A's turn to threaten a suit.

Instead of litigating, however, the companies respected a clause in their contract and headed into arbitration. Under normal circumstances, arbitration might take anywhere from 6 to 12 weeks, but in this case it ballooned into a five-year marathon, with five to six hours of testimony four or five days every single week. While the proceeding followed the customary rules of arbitration—in theory, extremely limited discovery and depositions—the judge in the case skirted convention by subpoenaing evidence, so that much of the time was actually spent in discovery nevertheless. In addition, lawyers on both sides began taking depositions, though they were careful not to use that word. One observer characterized the two sides as being driven by "fierce litigiousness, arrogance, and greed," and charges of attorney misconduct flew back and forth almost daily.

Eventually, the judge ruled against Company A, which promptly asked an appeals court to overturn the decision.

After that, both companies began to litigate in earnest. They are still fighting today, and the list of suits and countersuits grows longer every year. Company B is estimated to have laid out as much as $25 million a year to pursue its claims.

This depressing account graphically illustrates how an alternative method of dispute resolution can go wrong when the parties lack the commitment to make it work. Ingrained attitudes and belligerent corporate cultures worked against an equitable, agreeable outcome. In this case and in others we have seen, the chief obstacles were one or more of the following attitudes.

Winning is the only thing that matters. Few senior corporate managers are willing to forgo a chance to win a courtroom triumph. Here's the way a top lawyer at a major company puts it: "CEOs want to be able to take the other guy to the cleaners if they believe they're in the right, and they're going to bet the ranch if they have to." Often the case itself becomes less important than the principle involved. In the struggle between the electronics giants, for instance, the chief legal counsel for Company A declared, "If the other side continues its strategy of copying, I'm going to continue this strategy of suing."

It's one thing for the corporate general counsel to argue for arbitration when his or her company is the respondent or, as is often the case, when both parties are culpable to some degree. Under these circumstances, common sense urges negotiation to limit the extent of the claims. But when the company appears to be in the right, when millions in revenues are at stake, and when decision makers ache to go to the mat to prove their point, arguing for arbitration may strike some as foolish, if not downright disloyal.

ADR is only one alternative, not the method of choice. Most lawyers—and hence the companies they serve—still view ADR as the alternative rather than the primary or preferred method of settling disputes. Such companies see the procedure as a way of settling *Without the commitment of* peripheral, less important *top management, ADR* disputes, or, as in the *quickly turns into litigation-* electronics case, they sim- *in-disguise.* ply abandon it when they fail to get the result they want. In any event, they have not decided to make dispute avoidance and early resolution the prime mission of the legal department.

Even in companies where ADR has taken hold, there may be ways around the system. At Motorola, for example, at least ten circumstances can cause a dispute to be classified as an unsuitable candidate for early ADR, including "critical principle," "deterrent strategy," "the only issue is money," and "extremely complex factual issues." [1]

ADR isn't really all that different from litigation. Because few companies have made a serious commitment to ADR as a distinct system, and because there are very few rules governing it, the procedure is often allowed to become a litigation look-alike. Whenever that happens, the cost of ADR begins to approach the cost of the litigation that it's supposed to replace.

To cut down on attorney time, arbitration permits the parties to stipulate, or agree on, certain facts and virtually eliminate briefs, discovery, and the endless reliance on expert testimony and countertestimony. But the contending parties often waste prodigious quantities of time, money, and energy by reverting almost automatically to the habits of litigation. As happened in the electronics battle, lawyers make repetitious presentations of facts and legal arguments as if they were appearing before a judge rather than an arbitrator. They pursue discovery, file motions, and rely excessively on expert witnesses— exactly the way they would in a lawsuit. Outside the courtroom, lawyers grind out publicity favoring their cause. Moreover, arbitrators themselves contribute to the problem by handing down damage awards that are beyond reason and contractual limits. Sometimes, they even award punitive damages.

Adding to ADR's reputation as nothing more than litigation-in-disguise is the popularity of court-annexed ADR, which judges in federal jurisdictions often mandate after contestants have already begun to litigate. Not surprisingly, the parties tend to pursue the case as they began it—with a lot of hostility and all the expensive paraphernalia of a lawsuit—despite the judge's admonition to arbitrate. What's more, if either party objects to the arbitration decision, it can take the case back to the judge. Despite the drawbacks—high legal costs, lost time, lack of finality—some 65% of cases facilitated by the American Arbitration Association are court-annexed ADR.

ADR That Works

Ultimately, any company's view of arbitration and mediation boils down to whether or not top management insists on winning at all costs. In the case of Companies A and B, both of which had pledged to seek alternatives before taking court action, belligerence and litigious habits undermined good intentions. Both sides felt they had been wronged and wanted the antagonist to pay. A confrontational atmosphere tainted the action from the start, and the judge made matters worse. It is no easy matter to make ADR systematic and to give it top priority in resolving conflicts.

At NCR and many other companies we know of, including AT&T, US WEST, BankAmerica, and Chevron, top management has decided that winning at all costs is too expensive. These companies evaluate lawyers, contract managers, and paralegals not merely on lawsuits won or lost but also on disputes avoided, costs saved, and the crafting of solutions that preserve or even enhance existing relationships. The legal departments use quantified measures and objectives to reduce systematically the number of lawsuits pending, the amount of time and money spent on each conflict, and the amount of financial exposure. As a result of this kind of attention, NCR succeeds in resolving and closing more than 60% of filed cases within a year of their being opened.

NCR evaluates its lawyers not only on lawsuits won or lost but also on disputes avoided and relationships preserved.

NCR requires all of its commercial contracts to include a clause specifying ADR as the first, preferred method of settlement should a disagreement arise. (See "NCR's Standard Contract Clause" at the end of this article.) The corporate law department is built around a dispute avoidance and resolution process. Under this policy, staff ombudspersons (or, as NCR prefers to call them, ombuds) trained in problem solving, dispute avoidance, negotiation, and dispute resolution record and monitor all claims by or against the company. Each case is reviewed to ascertain whether it should be arbitrated or litigated. Performance measures ensure that the procedure has teeth.

At NCR, as well as at AT&T, an ombud analyzes each case at the outset in order to assess objectively the financial exposure posed by the claim. The written analysis, distributed to management, includes an ADR plan and suggestions on how to strengthen the relationship with the opponent. If the case can be handled

Few companies consider arbitration when they are convinced they're in the right.

through ADR at or below the calculated risk-exposure level, the company will proceed to resolve it without litigation. The overall aim is to resolve the contention efficiently with little expenditure of time and money.

The acid test of an organization's dedication to quiet dispute resolution comes when the company is the complainant. In this circumstance, few companies seriously consider negotiation. At NCR, however, management insists that resolution is preferable to litigation even when the company is convinced it's in the right.

In 1992, for example, NCR discovered that one of its suppliers had sent it computer boards that did not conform to specifications. NCR wanted to return the boards for a refund, but the vendor refused to cooperate on the grounds that NCR had not complained in a timely manner and that, in any event, the supplier could fix the defect. NCR did not want the goods repaired, because improved technology introduced in the interval had made the items virtually obsolete. NCR offered to compromise by returning the boards and claiming only a partial refund or a credit toward future orders of other products. The supplier declined to give a refund in any form, vowed to undertake a legal battle, and hired a large law firm.

Sticking to its policy, NCR declined to enter into litigation. Instead, it filed an arbitration demand. The vendor's counsel tried to throw the process off track in a number of different ways. First he objected to arbitration, then he protested the hearing venue, then he introduced a motion for discovery. But the American Arbitration Association dealt with those roadblocks, succeeded in scheduling an arbitration session, and, several days before the hearing, the parties settled.

In companies where a preference for ADR has taken hold, fresh approaches to conflict tend to bubble up almost on their own.

This case illustrates the routine though not negligible matters that arbitration handles particularly well. When each party's position has some merit, disputes over goods almost always end the same way: the party holding the cash decides to pay up before the case goes to trial. Here again, the prospect of arbitration quickly brought the case to its virtually predestined end, with a result almost certainly better than litigation could have achieved. Working through in-house counsel, NCR laid out less than $5,000. In contrast, because it retained counsel and dragged its feet on arbitration, the vendor spent more than $20,000, only to wind up with a result close to what NCR had proposed in the first place.

This case also illustrates the benefits that can stem from the single-minded avoidance of litigation. On the basis of its own analysis, NCR gave the supplier's claim some credence. NCR then made settlement offers built around credits to be applied to future business. When negotiation failed, the ombud pursued arbitration. Even after the hearing date had been set, the ombud continued doggedly to pursue negotiation and finally hit pay dirt.

In organizations where a preference for ADR has taken hold, fresh approaches to conflict tend to bubble up almost on their own. One example is the Toyota Reversal Arbitration Board mentioned earlier, which is a nonbinding mechanism to settle disagreements with its dealers.

Toyota's legal department set up the board at a time when negotiation was already a firmly established part of the company culture. The board had three distinctive features. First, it laid down rules for the arbitration process rather than allowing the process simply to develop on its own. Second, it made arbitration decisions binding on Toyota but allowed dealers to appeal. By underscoring the fairness of the procedure, this feature of the program has had the unexpected effect of actually increasing dealer acceptance of arbitration results. Third, it set up an open file of case histories, which has allowed Toyota and its dealers to cite relevant precedents and thus cut straight to a resolution of many disputes without laboring through the entire arbitration process. Because most disputes are similar, dealers with very little legal expertise can work through the details and find helpful patterns.

Toyota made arbitration decisions binding on itself but gave dealers the right to appeal.

A further positive outcome was Toyota's decision to amend the sales-credit program that had provoked much of the contention in the first place. Toyota's experience is typical of initiatives taken by many companies to avoid disputes by analyzing root causes and acting on the analysis—an indispensable aspect of the peaceful approach.

Make Sure It's Really Arbitration

Many companies have developed arbitration not so much to hold down as to disguise both costs and unnecessary procedures. As a result, arbitration is more expensive than it should be, and critics claim, with some justification, that ADR's cost-cutting ability is exaggerated. NCR has set up guidelines to deal with this problem. It has found that arbitration looks like, feels like, and works like arbitration when the parties are prepared to pursue the following goals.

Streamline the proceedings. The parties agree to stipulate undisputed facts and matters of law and to encourage the arbitrator to rule on disputed matters of law in summary form before hearing evidence. The arbitrator should specify which issues are most likely to generate disputes, and he or she should carefully avoid asking the parties to submit prehearing briefs on other issues, which is inevitably a waste of time and resources.

Limit the necessity for briefs. In some cases, no briefs are needed at all. For example, when NCR is the claimant in a hearing called to collect money on an account, the company usually cites the law orally or submits a photocopy of the relevant statute to the arbitrator. Even when briefs are appropriate—on developing matters of law, say, or where court decisions conflict—NCR has found that their greatest usefulness is in focusing attention on key issues. Arbitrators should be asked to identify the issues on which they want the parties to write briefs. NCR has even gone so far as to ask arbitrators to set page limits on briefs.

Participate in prehearing exchanges. Prehearing exchanges are invaluable in smoothing the way toward a resolution. The parties trade exhibits and witness lists, and discuss which items are important to the case and which peripheral. It is very important that these exchanges not resemble the discovery process typical of litigation; they should focus instead on documents to be used in the hearing. Prehearing exchanges often lead to a reduction in the witness lists and to having less important witnesses submit their testimony by affidavit or even by telephone.

Agree to limit damages. In order to restrict discussion and head off problems, NCR has drafted damage limitations into the standard ADR clause it includes in all commercial contracts. In many cases, there is or should be no legitimate argument about the amounts in dispute, which makes extensive damage proof unnecessary. Where possible, parties should stipulate the extent of damages and the arbitrator should rule on the reasonableness of damage limitations before hearing evidence. In more complicated cases, NCR may go so far as to exact agreement on a dollar floor or ceiling or on so-called baseball arbitration to keep the amount to a reasonable level. (In baseball arbitration, each party picks a figure and the arbitrator must choose one or the other.)

Instead of retaining opposing damage experts whose testimony conflicts, both parties should agree on a single, neutral expert.

Use experts selectively. In adversarial proceedings, each side typically tries to outexpert the other; in arbitration, a limit on the use of experts saves time and money. For instance, instead of retaining opposing damage experts whose testimonies are likely to conflict, it makes good sense for both parties to agree on a single, neutral expert. This person's report puts pressure on the two sides to negotiate, whereas divergent, partisan reports encourage opponents to dig in and harden their positions.

NCR has used the "neutral expert" effectively in other situations as well, including accident investigation and reconstruction, auditing and accounting, and technology issues. One effective use of expert testimony is to ask each party and the arbitrator to submit key questions for the expert to examine. In some areas—technology, for example—the expert can play a role in root-cause analysis by recommending improvements in products or practices. This is a much more constructive activity than merely offering a partisan opinion.

The standard ADR clause inserted into all NCR commercial contracts has many features that help ensure that arbitration will really be arbitration and not camouflaged litigation. Among them are guidelines on the qualifications of the arbitrator, empowerment of the arbitrator to grant injunctive relief, an agreement that challenges to arbitration or award decisions be governed by federal arbitration law (and that the challenger must pay costs and fees if it loses), and limitations on discovery.

The Process Systematized

Boosting commitment to ADR and avoiding the trap of litigation-in-disguise are both important steps in the effort to replace confrontation with negotiation. The essential third step is to create a systematic process that mandates ADR as the first step in every legal action. At NCR, the Dispute Avoidance Resolution Process, called DARP, begins when the ombud reviews the dispute, regardless of whether NCR has initiated the complaint or another party has named NCR as respondent.

By DARP rules, every dispute is entered into a PC database within 24 hours of its inception, and everyone at NCR who needs to know is notified, from those involved in the complaint to those who may help to resolve it. Within three days, NCR notifies opposing counsel that it is addressing the problem with a view toward peaceful resolution.

Another distinctive feature of NCR's system is the way its law department monitors the process and measures the performance of its ombud according to the number of issues resolved, the number resolved without litigation, the quality and permanence of solutions, the efforts made to analyze disputes and identify ways of preventing similar occurrences in the future, and the precise amount of time and money saved through efficient ADR.

To see how this system works, let's follow an actual dispute between NCR's computer systems division and a big passenger carrier.

The division's installation of computer hardware went well. Then came a glitch: while the contract called on NCR to supply one repeated-use, or *multipass*, ribbon cassette for each printer, it turned out that no vendor could deliver a multipass ribbon to the specs of the printers designed for the project. The project team, which included representatives of both companies, accepted NCR's proposal to furnish several single-pass ribbons per printer instead.

Several months later, some executives of the carrier raised the matter of the multipass ribbon once again. Despite NCR's explanations, they referred back to the wording of the original contract in meeting after meeting, and in increasingly hostile tones. Soon the amicable relationship had deteriorated, and each meeting became a rehash of previous encounters. The customer stopped making payment on the contract, to the tune of some $250,000. On the heels of this action came a letter from the customer's in-house counsel, who wrote that the carrier wanted relief not for the undelivered ribbons but for the added costs over several years of using the single-pass cassettes, amounting to several hundred thousand dollars.

A healthy business relationship had gone sour over a small matter. At this point, the problem could easily have become irretrievable, but NCR's Dispute Avoidance Resolution Process succeeded in untangling the mess. DARP's basic features should form the foundation of any such system.

The system kicked in immediately. As soon as the customer's letter arrived, DARP went into play. The ombud (in this case, an in-house lawyer) immediately telephoned the customer's counsel to pinpoint the nature of the problem and discuss the contract provisions in dispute. A paralegal well versed in DARP procedure was assigned to investigate the situation and look for possible solutions (including a review of alternative sources of multipass

To NCR executives, maintaining a relationship with the customer was more important than the letter of the contract.

ribbons). The ombud had the contract and some key related documents collected, analyzed, and summarized. She also interviewed several NCR employees who had played critical roles in the history of the dispute.

The ombud quickly narrowed the issues. The ombud discussed the problem with the customer's representatives and reviewed the contract's dispute resolution clause. The two sides soon reached agreement on the chronology of the project, and they stipulated a list of events and the specifics of the contract. They then decided to bypass the project team, with all its emotional baggage, and put the matter into the hands of senior managers.

An executive-level negotiation was tried first without lawyers or the managers directly involved in the dispute. NCR wanted to make clear to the customer that it valued the relationship and that the matter of the contract was subordinate to maintaining that tie. The customer was similarly well intentioned. So the two sides agreed on a negotiation between executives, without lawyers or project managers, although a few people acquainted with the project and the contracts were on hand in the room. Each side was represented by an executive with decision-making authority who had no previous connection with the project.

Preparation was painstaking. The key to successful negotiation is preparation. The ombud worked long hours with the participants well ahead of the meeting. Each participant received a notebook containing the contract itself, interview summaries, and lists of essential stipulated facts. The ombud and her team also came up with a litigation risk analysis that laid out the economic exposure for both sides and brainstormed a variety of solutions that acknowledged the customer's interests as well as NCR's.

The tone of the negotiation was positive. After agreeing to the facts of the case, the executives traded compliments. The customer's representative declared that his company was well satisfied with the system, and the NCR representative made it clear that his company wanted to have the customer's continuing business. The two executives considered many possible

> *Litigation tends to produce only winners and losers—not solutions to joint problems.*

solutions and agreed on one of them after only a few hours of talk. That solution involved neither a financial settlement nor provision of multipass cassettes but an alteration in the design of the printer so that it could use a different and commonly available multipass ribbon.

NCR estimated that this method of resolving the dispute saved it as much as $200,000 and that it saved the carrier a similar amount. Litigation would have run the costs much higher while expending valuable internal resources. Even then, the confrontation would only have produced a winner and a loser, not a solution to the joint problem of the ribbons.

No ADR plan will ever prevent all litigation, but none will come close without the wholehearted commitment of company management. At NCR, with that kind of commitment firmly in place, there are really three keys to success. The first is time. Disputes age badly, so the DARP system is designed to report, analyze, address, and resolve them before they can fester into litigation.

The second is persistence. NCR's ombuds not only act quickly, they also act thoroughly. They notify all relevant parties, they examine history and background in detail, they go out of their way to understand their opponent's point of view, they take great pains in preparing their negotiations, and, most important, they don't give up. They generate a range of potential solutions, and when one form of ADR fails to resolve the problem, they invariably propose another.

The third reason why DARP works is that NCR continuously reevaluates and improves the system. The company subjects each case to a postmortem, refines its procedures accordingly, and adds to its stock of insights. DARP is now the beneficiary of years of trial and error in ADR proceedings.

Alternatives to Litigation

ADR PROCEDURES FALL INTO two general categories. The first, arbitration, most resembles litigation. The second category consists of various forms of negotiation, including mediation, settlement conferences, summary jury trials, and minitrials. Then there are hybrids, like mediation/arbitration, when issues that cannot be settled through mediation are put in binding arbitration for resolution.

The principal ADR procedures in use today include:

Arbitration. Procedures similar to those in a regular trial replace the binding decision of a judge or jury with that of another third party, such as an arbitrator, referee, or private judge. Often parties have a clause in their contract committing them to arbitration of disputes arising from their business together. Typically, they adopt procedures recommended by the American Arbitration Association.

Settlement Conference. Sometimes a preliminary meeting of the parties can settle differences early on. Disputants themselves often initiate such a conference, or counsel or outside consultants bring the parties together. Usually, each side is represented by an executive with decision-making authority but no previous connection with the project.

Mediation. Whereas arbitration imposes solutions, mediation helps parties resolve their own disputes. The mediator's functions vary depending on the personalities and wishes of the disputants, the nature of the issues, and the personality and skills of the mediator. Mediators can play many roles: getting participants to talk to each other, setting the agenda, helping disputants understand their problems, and suggesting possible solutions.

Summary Jury Trial. Litigants are often unable to settle their disputes quickly because they have very different expectations of how a jury will view their claims. An SJT gives them a nonbinding indication of how their claims might actually be received. Opposing lawyers select a small jury, a judge gives preliminary instructions on the law, and everything proceeds just as in a real trial, but with a limited number of witnesses and a restricted time frame for each party.

Minitrial. The disputants usually initiate this procedure themselves, and formats vary. Typically, minitrials involve one high-level executive from each side (someone not previously involved with the issue) and one neutral adviser. Before the process, the parties exchange documents and briefs, and they may engage in some discovery and take witnesses' testimony. They also agree on format, timing, and procedures. During the minitrial, each side has an allotted time to present its case, and attendees can comment and ask questions. Afterward, the executives may be able to settle the dispute on their own, or they may turn to the neutral person for advice. The whole process usually takes from one to four days.

The Center for Public Resources Policy Statement

THE CENTER FOR PUBLIC RESOURCES, INC., has published the following suggested corporate policy statement for signature by a company's CEO and chief legal officer:

We recognize that for many business disputes there is a less expensive, more effective method of resolution than the traditional lawsuit. Alternative dispute resolution (ADR) procedures involve collaborative techniques which can often spare businesses the high costs of litigation.

In recognition of the foregoing, we subscribe to the following statement of principle on behalf of our company and its domestic subsidiaries:

In the event of a business dispute between our company and another company which has made or will make a similar statement, we are prepared to explore with that party resolution of the dispute through negotiation or ADR techniques before pursuing full-scale litigation. If either party believes that the dispute is not suitable for ADR techniques, or if such techniques do not produce results satisfactory to the disputants, either party may proceed with litigation.

NCR's Standard Contract Clause

IN THE EVENT OF any controversy or claim, whether based on contract, tort, statute, or other legal or equitable theory (including but not limited to any claim of fraud, misrepresentation, or fraudulent inducement), arising out of or related to this agreement, or any subsequent agreement between the parties ("dispute"), and if the dispute cannot be resolved by negotiation, the parties agree to submit the dispute to mediation by a mediator mutually selected by the parties. If the parties are unable to agree upon a mediator, then the mediator shall be appointed by the American Arbitration Association. In any event, the mediation shall take place within thirty (30) days of the date that a party gives the other party written notice of its desire to mediate the dispute.

If not thus resolved, the disputes shall be resolved by arbitration pursuant to this section and the then-current rules and supervision of the American Arbitration Association.

The duties to mediate and arbitrate shall extend to any other office, employee, shareholder, principal, agent trustee in bankruptcy or otherwise, affiliate, subsidiary, third-party beneficiary, or guarantor of a party hereto making or defending any claim which would otherwise be subject to this section.

The arbitration shall be held in the headquarters city of the party not initiating the claim before a single arbitrator who is knowledgeable in business information and electronic data processing systems. The arbitrator's decision and award shall be final and binding and may be entered in any court having jurisdiction thereof. The arbitrator shall not have the power to award punitive, exemplary, or consequential damages, or any damages excluded by or in excess of any damage limitations expressed in this agreement or any subsequent agreement between the parties.

In order to prevent irreparable harm, the arbitrator may grant temporary or permanent injunctive or other equitable relief for the protection of property rights.

Issues of arbitrability shall be determined in accordance with the federal substantive and procedural laws relating to arbitration; all other aspects of the agreement shall be interpreted in accordance with and the arbitrator shall apply and be bound to follow the substantive laws of the state of _____. Each party shall bear its own attorney's fees associated with negotiation, mediation, and arbitration, and other costs and expenses shall be borne as provided by the rules of the American Arbitration Association.

If court proceedings to stay litigation or compel arbitration are necessary, the party who unsuccessfully opposes such proceedings shall pay all associated costs, expenses, and attorney's fees which are reasonably incurred by the other party.

The arbitrator may order the parties to exchange copies of nonrebuttal exhibits and copies of witness lists in advance of the arbitration hearing. However, the arbitrator shall have no other power to order discovery or depositions unless and then only to the extent that all parties otherwise agree in writing.

Neither a party, witness, or the arbitrator may disclose the facts of the underlying dispute or the contents or results of any negotiation, mediation, or arbitration hereunder without prior written consent of all parties, unless and then only to the extent required to enforce or challenge the negotiated agreement or the arbitration award, as required by law, or as necessary for financial and tax reports and audits.

No party may bring a claim or action, regardless of form, arising out of or related to this agreement, including any claim of fraud, misrepresentation, or fraudulent inducement, more than one year after the cause of action accrues, unless the injured party cannot reasonably discover the basic facts supporting the claim within one year.

Notwithstanding anything to the contrary in this section, in the event of alleged violation of a party's property or equitable rights (including but not limited to unauthorized disclosure of confidential information), that party may seek temporary injunctive relief from any court of competent jurisdiction pending appointment of an arbitrator. The party requesting such relief shall simultaneously file a demand for mediation and arbitration of the dispute, and shall request the American Arbitration Association to proceed under its rules for expedited procedures. In no event shall any such court-ordered temporary injunctive relief continue for more than thirty (30) days.

If any part of this section is held to be unenforceable, it shall be severed and shall not affect either the duties to mediate and arbitrate hereunder or any other part of this section.

Notes

1. Richard H. Weise, *Representing the Corporate Client: Designs for Quality* (New York: Prentice Hall, 1991).

Originally published in May–June 1994
Reprint 94301

Authors' note: The authors wish to thank Douglas N. Dickson of Price Waterhouse for his assistance in researching and writing this article.

About the Contributors

JOHN R. ALLISON is the Mary and John Spence Centennial Professor of Business Administration at the Graduate School of Business at the University of Texas, Austin. His research and teaching interests include intellectual property protection, employment regulation, and the design and evaluation of dispute resolution and decision-making systems in regulatory programs.

ROBERT R. BLAKE was formerly the Chairman of Scientific Methods, Inc. Upon his retirement in 1997, he sold the company to Grid International, Inc. and continues to work with them as a consultant. He has lectured at Harvard, Oxford, and Cambridge Universities, and has worked on special extended assignments at the Tavistock Clinic, London, as a Fulbright Scholar. He has served as a consultant to governments, industries, Fortune 500 companies, and universities in 40 countries. He and Jane Mouton coauthored several books including *The New Managerial Grid*, *The Secretary Grid*, *Productivity: The Human Side*, and *The Academic Administrator Grid*.

TODD B. CARVER is a Senior Attorney at US West, Inc. in Denver, Colorado. Prior to his position at US West, he was a Senior Attorney at NCR Corporation and an Adjunct Professor of Law at the University of Dayton Law School. He is currently on the Board of Advisers for the school. He has received a variety of community service awards and has served in leadership positions for Preservation Daytona Inc., Boy Scouts of America, and the U.S. Selective Service Commission. He has published several articles that have appeared in professional journals such as *Harvard Business Review, Dispute Resolution Journal,* and *University of Dayton Law Review.*

DANNY ERTEL is a Founding Partner of Vantage Partners LLC, a consulting spin-off of the Harvard Negotiation Project dedicated to helping organizations around the world more effectively manage their most valuable and important relationships. His practice is focused on helping clients build the necessary systems, structures, tools, skills, and mind-sets to consistently create and capture value through collaboration. He served as a Senior Researcher at the Harvard Negotiation Project, taught Negotiation at the University of Toronto Law Faculty, and practiced law with the firm of Debevoise & Plimpton. He is the author or editor of three books including *Beyond Arbitration,* which won the 1992 CPR Legal Program Book Award, and *Getting Ready To Negotiate,* with Roger Fisher. He can be reached at dertel@cmi-vantage.com.

SALLY FOWLER is Assistant Professor in Strategic Management and International Business at the University of Victoria Faculty of Business in British Columbia. Her research interests focus on strategic decision making, top management teams, and stakeholder analysis. Prior to her completing her Ph.D., she worked for 11 years in commercial banking and ten 10 years in management consulting and was a Principal of the Washington, D.C. office of Deloitte & Touche.

At the time his article appeared in *Harvard Business Review,* THOMAS C. KEISER was a Senior Vice President at the Forum Corporation, a training and education consulting firm in Boston, MA.

IDALENE F. KESNER is the Frank P. Popoff Professor of Strategic Management at Indiana University's Kelley School of

Business. She is also Director of the school's Consulting Academy and teaches in the areas of strategic management, crisis management, change management, and management consulting. She has taught in over 60 different executive education programs, and she has served as a consultant for many different national and international firms. Her research interests focus on corporate boards of directors, chief executive succession, corporate governance, and mergers and acquisitions. She currently serves on the board of directors for two U.S. firms and one Canadian firm.

JANE S. MOUTON was the President and Cofounder of Scientific Methods, Inc., and was codeveloper with Robert R. Blake of the concepts of the Managerial Grid. She was an Associate of the American Psychological Association, a Diplomate in Industrial and Organizational Psychology and the American Board of Psychology, and a member of the American Association for the Advancement of Science. In addition to her work in the area of organizational development, she engaged in research on conformity, dynamics of win-lose conflict, and creative decision making. She and Robert R. Blake coauthored several books including *The New Managerial Grid*, *The Secretary Grid*, *Productivity: The Human Side*, and *The Academic Administrator Grid*.

At the time his article appeared in *Harvard Business Review*, WARREN H. SCHMIDT was a Senior Lecturer in Behavioral Sciences at the University of California, Los Angeles. Besides writing extensively in the fields of human relations, leadership, and conference planning, Mr. Schmidt also wrote the screenplay for the film "Is It Always Right to Be Right?" which won an Academy Award in 1970.

At the time his article appeared in *Harvard Business Review*, ROBERT TANNENBAUM was a Professor of Development of

Human Systems at the University of California, Los Angeles Graduate School of Management. He was a Consulting Editor of the *Journal of Applied Behavioral Science* and a coauthor of *Leadership and Organization.*

ALBERT A. VONDRA is a Partner with Pricewaterhouse-Coopers in Cleveland, Ohio, and has 20 years of experience in public accounting, including a two year international assignment in Athens, Greece. He has in-depth experience in financial analysis from a broad business background in directing audit/review engagements, internal control reviews, computer system audits, acquisition and merger reviews, fraud investigations, business valuations, and dispute and damage analysis. He also has extensive experience as engagement partner to over 100 publicly held and private companies. He has published numerous articles in the areas of accounting, auditing, and dispute analysis, and authored his firm's national guidelines in conducting arbitration engagements involving complex accounting disputes. His publications have appeared in professional journals such as *Harvard Business Review*, *Journal of Accountancy*, *Ohio CPA Journal*, *Financial Executive*, and many others.

SUZY WETLAUFER, formerly of the international management consulting firm Bain & Company, is a Senior Editor of the *Harvard Business Review*, specializing in the area of leadership, teams, and organizational psychodynamics. In addition to "After the Layoffs, What Next?" and "Leadership When There is No One to Ask," she is the author or coauthor of numerous HBR pieces including, "What's Killing the Creativity at Coolburst?" and "A Question of Color."

Note: *Information provided within each article about the contributors to case studies was applicable at the time of original publication.*

Index

NIAGARA COLLEGE LRC

274019